PUNCHING
The # SUN

Heb 12:1 !

Run the Race !.

Rob

PUNCHING
The SUN

CHARLES R. ROBINSON

TATE PUBLISHING
AND ENTERPRISES, LLC

Published by Tate Publishing & Enterprises, LLC
127 E. Trade Center Terrace | Mustang, Oklahoma 73064 USA
1.888.361.9473 | www.tatepublishing.com

Tate Publishing is committed to excellence in the publishing industry. The company reflects the philosophy established by the founders, based on Psalm 68:11,
"The Lord gave the word and great was the company of those who published it."

Book design copyright © 2012 by Tate Publishing, LLC. All rights reserved.
Cover design by Jan Sunday Quilaquil
Interior design by Jomel Pepito

Published in the United States of America

ISBN: 978-1-62147-574-3
1. Religion, Christian Life, Inspirational
2. Fiction, Biographical
12.10.22

DEDICATION

Jonah Richard Medina was born sixteen weeks premature on November 15, 2011. He crossed over to be with the Lord three days later. His time with us was very short, but his presence still lingers in our hearts. Jonah departed with his arms lifted high above his head in triumph as he raced across the finished line of life. How did he come to know these actions at such an early age? We really don't know, but this is the vision his mother saw in her spirit as he slipped from physical life with us to eternal life with the Lord. In three days he stepped into the lives of thousands of saints around the world as they prayed for his life. Now he has accomplished what everyone desires. That is to live forever in the presence of the Lord. This book is dedicated to you. You have overcome!

I will see you again, soon.
Grandpa

ACKNOWLEDGMENTS

*W*ords are insufficient to express my gratitude to my partner, best friend, and spouse. She spent countless hours proofing this work. Her constant encouragement and insights truly made this work a partnership. Thank you, Eloisa. A book has happened!

To the many great people who told me to write a book, I thank you for encouraging me to do so.

TABLE OF CONTENTS

INTRODUCTION

*I*t was chaos! Drill sergeants yelling for everyone to get off the bus and get in something they called a "formation." The biggest sergeant of them all was standing right in the path of everyone getting off the bus. Everyone was expected to dismount this old crate they called "transportation" quickly and do so with this mountain of a man standing smack in their way. No one dared bump into him lest they find themselves doing pushups for the rest of their life, or so they were told. Rob thought, *Good Lord, what in the world have I got myself into now?* Later they learned these tactics of controlled chaos were carefully planned to form them into soldiers ready for combat in eight short weeks. Some men refused to be reformed and were discharged in a few days. The rest were totally broken and rebuilt into entirely different creatures in a few weeks. Most soldiers learned quickly to do as instructed and not let the sun set while doing it. Word spread quickly that "it was a head game"—a method the Army used called basic training to reform a man, to rebuild an individual with the mind set of courage and confidence instilled so deeply that they could face the dangers of war and not run.

They developed tough attitudes, like if they told them to run one mile, they would say they were ready to run two. If the command was for ten pushups, twenty was the goal. Just don't let them break you down to a crying, sniffling mess. Some were volunteers, but most of the men were drafted into the military. They were all taught that they could do more than they thought they could. They were told to push harder and be stronger, wiser, and faster than the enemy, or they would die in combat. They were told to never ever give up, run until they dropped and then crawl until they could run again.

Running was not what Rob looked forward to each day. In fact, Rob did just about anything to get out of running. He spent years thinking up ways of getting away from having to run. In his mind, he did not sign up in the Army to run. Rob just wanted to work at his job, mechanics, and he did not consider running a part of the job. As for the basic training thought of running two if they asked for one, well, that was basic training. When it was over, Rob tried hard not to think of those things. Now that Rob was on his own, away from the drill sergeants, he could live any way he wanted. Rob was determined to answer and live for no one but himself.

That is the way Rob viewed his Christian beginnings, as well. Rob thought was that his parents sent him to Sunday school to learn good habits. In his opinion, that was finished. That season of life now past. Parental control was now over. Rob was free to live as he pleased. After all, he was old enough to be an adult; it was time he started to think for himself. What Rob didn't realize was that all those Sunday school teachings were meant for walking with the Lord every day...until.

In 1986 one of his younger brothers died in an accident, and his life took on a big change. God spoke to Rob of his life and how he was living. Rob knew he did not line up with God's Word in any way. Rob realized he was not going to be pleased with the outcome at the end of his life. To state it plainly, Rob did not believe he would enter heaven's gates, and he was afraid to face God on any level. Rob realized that he needed help and gave God control of his life. Rob quickly came to understand that life held much more than he had ever dreamed. God began challenging him in every aspect of his life. In what God expected of him as a husband, father of three children, and a soldier in the military. Today, many years later, He is still at work in all those areas, except now, Rob is father to four and grandfather to five plus a spiritual father to many in the army of God.

God began to teach Rob that walking through life is like running a marathon. Of course we know that life is a lot longer than a twenty-six mile marathon. One thing they hold in common is that both are hinged on endurance. We cannot run half the marathon and claim the prize for running the whole. The run of life is much the same. We will not be able to live a haphazard life and claim we lived it to the fullest. Likewise, those who start with Christ and don't finish with Him might be greatly disappointed when they arrive at the finish. Just saying we know who Jesus is but never developing a walk-through-life relationship with Him may not be enough. Does He know our name? That is a better question. After all, it is Jesus who calls for us to "come" when we enter the final storm of life. We cannot choose the time when we go to Heaven; that decision is the Lord's. To those who finish, it says in the book of Revelation, 3:21-22 (KJV), "To him that overcometh will I grant to sit with me in my throne, even as I also overcame, and am set down with my Father in his throne. He that hath an ear, let him hear what the Spirit saith to the churches."

Life is a marathon that we all have been given to run. How we run and who we run with in life makes all the difference in how we finish. Determine now to finish the race.

AN INVITATION TO RUN

*E*arly in his life, young Rob dreamed of going places and doing things that he had heard that some men do. He wanted to live like Fest Parker, TV's Daniel Boone, and the Family Robinson, who explored outer space, another TV program. These television programs showed people who overcame all sorts of obstacles. Rob believed deep down he too, could overcome any obstacle and bare any hardship that came before him. What Rob wanted most was to be well thought of, respected, and sought after for his wisdom and strength. He desired to be the best and have the best. He was determined to somehow work his way into wearing these crowns of glory by using his personality and physical abilities. Whatever got in his way, he would find a way around it and keep moving toward his own destiny. School was something he thought to be taking too much time as he raced forward to do great things. Rob's way of thinking led him to drop out of school and join the US Army at a very young age.

"Outside! Outside, everybody up and outside for PT! Five minutes!" Drill sergeants, demanded loudly as they pounded the doors, opening each room without invitation, kicking bunk beds, and flipping on the lights.

"Everyone get up! You cannot sleep all day. You are in the Army now!" DIs growling, "You're in US Army now!" Somehow these commands were not lining up with Rob's initial vision of fun and adventure while serving in the US Army. "Things have to get done, and we have places to go. Get up!" the DI's yelled again.

Rob's eyes snapped opened. His body was in motion, but his mind was not responding very well. "What...? What is happening? What time is it? Why the urgency?" Rob's eyes began to focus from the attack they received when the bright lights were turned on pretty much without warning. Someone said it was still dark outside. Indeed it was dark—so dark it was hard to see out the window. Stumbling toward the latrine—*bathroom* in military language—everyone stood in line, waiting to use the sinks and every other facility the latrine had. Three of those minutes already wasted just trying to get his eyes open. Rob opted to use the restroom and forgo the oral hygiene. Maybe if his mouth stunk really badly, these get-in-your-face drill sergeants would not want to get too close to him. It seemed like good reasoning at the time, but it didn't work. The DI's breath was worse. It billowed out with the smell of too much strong coffee.

Outside, everyone began to form up into what the Army called a *formation*. This is where the soldiers stood side by side in something called *ranks*. Three ranks standing behind the first form a *platoon* of four ranks. It was so dark they could hardly see the first rank that was only a couple of steps away. "It's four thirty," someone said. No wonder it was still dark!

Out in front somewhere in the dark was a DI instructing everyone to begin the daily exercise. Everyone did some stretching and then started a series of upper-body-building exercises. "Hands up," he commanded. "Reach for the sun!"

What sun? Rob thought. The sun, he knew, would not be up for hours.

"Reach for the sun and keep your arms up!" DIs shouted. In moments Rob's arms began to burn. The DI kept talking. "Keep them up! Keep reaching for the sun!" He continued talking as everyone held their hands up. Muscles were burning under the strain of holding their arms and hands up for so long. The DI seemed to delight in the troop's struggle. Taunting with comments of how everyone would get to run as soon as the sun punched through the darkness.

Oh joy, Rob thought. *They woke us up at four in the morning to come outside and wait with our hands held in the air for the sun to rise.* Rob was sure there were other exercises that they did at that time, but this drill of just standing still and holding one's hands up and out in the air was like torture. The length of time with his hands over his head caused his muscles to weary. In order to keep his hands up, he made a fist, forcing his body to perform under the strain. It looked a lot like he was punching the sun.

When their arms began to fall, commands came quickly from the DIs to "Get those arms up, soldier!" Private Rob was actually relieved when the sun finally rose. Even thou Rob hated to run, running was better than holding his arms up in the air.

Days went by pretty fast and he graduated from basic training and on to his specialized training school. For Rob the years went by fairly swiftly as well. Private Rob had progressed up through the ranks to staff sergeant and then went on to become a Warrant Officer. The Army and life in general held many challenges that Rob overcame but none quite so demanding as the Marine Corp Marathon.

Running a twenty-six mile marathon was not on Chief Warrant Officer Rob's list of things to do in life until his US Army Battalion Commander stepped into the office one morning and said, "Chief, it would be great to run the Marine Corps Marathon in Washington, DC, together!" *Stunned* is a good word to use here. Did Rob really hear the colonel invite him to run? Chief Rob was winding down his Army career. He had just a couple of more years to go until retirement. He definitely was not excited about running anywhere unless there was a good reason. Something like the house being on fire could be a good reason. Running twenty-six miles just so he could boast of running somehow did not have that ring of good reason. In fact, it sounded like a bad idea.

The thoughts that ran through the chief's mind at that very moment had much more to do with running away from this invitation than embracing the colonel's request. Rob did not want to run around his *desk*, let alone twenty-six miles. However, seventeen years in the US Army had developed a keen sense of discernment when addressed by authorities of rank. His quick, respectful, and carefully worded response was, "Yes, sir, it would be great." Then there was a stammered disclaimer that sounded something like, "A run like this will take some additional training if anyone hopes to accomplish running twenty-six miles without stopping." The colonel quickly agreed that help and time would be available. It was easy to see the colonel was excited about this running event. It was also clear to see he was willing to sacrifice some day-to-day duties in order to fulfill the dream he had of leading an Army team in the Marine Corps Marathon. It was not the best time to refuse the invitation. Colonels as well as other leaders in authority usually spoke in tones that sounded like suggestions but carried the weight of direct orders. Technically, the colonel could not have made Rob run a twenty-six-mile marathon; it was, after all, an extra curricular activity. But telling the colonel what he could and could not do would not be wise— he was the boss. Rob wanted to be thought of as a team player, part of the organization. He did not want to start an authority contest between the colonel and himself. He wasn't too sure he wanted to run either. The colonel's visit to Rob's office indicated he had confidence in Rob's abilities and desired him on the team. By refusing the invitation right away, Rob thought he could have initiated a rift between them. He needed time to think of a really good reason for not fulfilling the colonel's request. Besides, not taking time to consider the colonel's invitation would have been disrespectful.

After a few days of pondering the pros and cons of this request, Rob began to accept the challenge rather than reject the invitation. After all, if others could accomplish a run such as this, why not him? The one to gain the most from the training was going to be him. Rob began to think running a twenty-six mile marathon might have some benefits. Running a marathon is something very few people ever accomplish and it would give him something to boast about.

It was in Rob's character to work just as hard doing the task the colonel wanted even if he didn't get his own way. Hard work, good, thought-out suggestions, and respect always proved to be beneficial in exchanges with any authority. Often we must give in at the moment in order to benefit at the next. Chief Rob's history was not always so diplomatic. In his earlier years, he was much more self-centered. In those days he would have stood toe to toe with his superiors and emptied his thoughts on how he felt about their instructions. He might have had to do the task, but it would be clear to everyone that it was not done willingly. In the process he created a rift between himself and others hindering any future favor between them. This type of behavior prompted an older officer one day to challenge him by saying, "It appears you think yourself wiser than your superior. Why don't you study and work your way into the position he holds? Then you can make the decisions and hope others will follow you." Rob took the challenge that day, and eighteen months later the US Army took the stripes off his arms and pinned bars on his shoulders. He was now in charge! Leading was more difficult than he imagined. Rob found out quickly he needed good people to follow his lead. Rob also found out that he did not know everything and needed others who had wisdom in the areas where he was lacking. Many of these persons filled with the wisdom he lacked were below his rank. The men and women that caught his attention and won his respect did so with their display of respect toward him.

God's Word, the Bible, states that "All things work together for the good of those who love Him, and are called according to His purpose" (Romans 8:28, KJV, paraphrased). Rob took this verse to mean that regardless of what is happening at the present at some point in time, now or in the future, the task given will do something good for those who love God. This truth may be harder to walk out than to talk about, but it is true. Submitting to the run and the authority that directed him was going to be a blessing and would continue to be in the future.

The Lord God has chosen to speak to us in a soft, invitational manner. He is the highest of all rank and authority. He is God, and above Him there is no other. His approach of love and respect toward us is often misunderstood or ignored all together. Scripture reveals that God desires great things in our lives but leaves the decision to us as to whether we want His involvement or not. He gives us choices. His offer of living victoriously may be enjoyed by embracing His precepts that are recorded in the Bible. Some may think God is out to take everything that's fun away from us. To the contrary, God is waiting to add to our lives. These additions often will be physical changes and will always include spiritual enlightenment.

Life is very much like a marathon. It's a run that requires strength and endurance. Life is not how fast we live or how much stuff we collect. Life should be about quality and what we have done to better life for others as well as ourselves. Of course where we finish life is of utmost importance. The best recorded account of this principle is found in the book of Luke.

> There was a certain rich man, which was clothed in purple and fine linen, and fared sumptuously every day: And there was a certain beggar named Lazarus, which was laid at his gate, full of sores, And desiring to be fed with the crumbs which fell from the rich man's table: moreover the dogs came and licked his sores. And it came to pass, that the beggar died, and was carried by the angels into Abraham's bosom: the rich man also died, and was buried; And in hell he lift up his eyes, being in torments, and seeth Abraham afar off, and Lazarus in his bosom. And he cried and said, Father Abraham, have mercy on me, and send Lazarus that he may dip the tip of his finger in water, and cool my

tongue; for I am tormented in this flame. But
Abraham said, Son, remember that thou in thy
lifetime receivedst thy good things, and likewise
Lazarus evil things: but now he is comforted,
and thou art tormented. And beside all this,
between us and you there is a great gulf fixed: so
that they which would pass from hence to you
cannot; neither can they pass to us, that would
come from thence. Then he said, I pray thee
therefore, father, that thou wouldest send him
to my father's house: For I have five brethren;
that he may testify unto them, lest they also
come into this place of torment. Abraham saith
unto him, They have Moses and the prophets;
let them hear them. And he said, Nay, father
Abraham: but if one went unto them from the
dead, they will repent. And he said unto him, If
they hear not Moses and the prophets, neither
will they be persuaded, though one rose from
the dead.

Luke 16: 19-31, KJV

Here we find a man who apparently collected all
the best things in life, but at death he abruptly realized
that he missed what was most important. That missing
element is a relationship with God. To have riches
without God is to miss the most important and most
valuable thing in life. Contrast this to people who have
God. They always feel like they are rich and realize
they also have more than enough. Material possessions
just won't fill that place in life that is meant for a
relationship with God. It all boils down to the real
answer for enjoying life is found in relationships with

the Lord and His people, not things. Attempting to live without the Lord is a set up for failure, despair, and heartache. It is far better to be poor physically than to be poor spiritually. The wealthiest people on earth may not have a lot of money or things that money can buy, but they possess joy, hope, and comfort in God, who they know truly loves them. Some of the poorest people have things that own them and troubles that overwhelm them, and they struggle constantly with the fear of losing the stuff they have collected. God has purpose and a destiny for each individual that is more important than owning stuff.

God has quietly invited everyone to run the race of life with Him. God has the ability to see the beginning and the end of our lives. Both time and space are laid out like a map before Him. If we were seated in a position high above an ongoing race, we could see the participants lining up at the start and moving through the course to the finish. We would see the entire life span of the participants in the race. From this vantage point, one would know the location of each person, where they had been, and what they are going to do at any given moment during the race. We have a God that does more than see our entire world. He knows where we began, and He knows where we are and each turn we will take at any time. He has knowledge of what we will do next. He can also see the intents of our heart before they become actions. He is aware of the good and bad times we will encounter. When life picks us up or knocks us down, He can see each event and how we will respond to it. We, however, can only see the past and the point where we stand presently. What is next is a mystery. Where, when, and how our life ends we may not know, but God knows every detail all the way through to the end. Now think about that for a moment. Once we realize that God has this ability to see our past, present, and future, doesn't it make perfect sense to submit to His leadership? He is not demanding. He does not get in our face, shouting commands that we follow Him. Instead, He quietly suggests we take His help.

We all are presently running the race of life—a *marathon*. Will it be with God or without Him? He desires to be with us in good times and bad. Isn't that what most of us want—to have someone that stands by our side constantly, to love us when we are unlovable, to help us when we get ourselves in trouble, and to rejoice with us in our victories?

God sent His Son, Jesus, to present a special invitation to all of us to come and follow Him straight toward the kingdom of God. In Exodus 19:5 (KJV), God presented to Israel a covenant to be His people. He calls those who follow Him a peculiar treasure. That word, *peculiar*, includes the meaning *special*. Most of us can grasp the idea of treating treasure with a little extra care. Because God's word is everlasting, He called Israel and is still calling people to Himself that He can treat with a little extra care—special!

Rejecting this special care offer from the Lord opens up the door to receive the opposite. On this side of death, life may be good, but on the other side, we will find the conditions extremely unfavorable. King

David warns in Psalm 55:23 (KJV), "But thou, O God, shalt bring them down....... men shall not live out half their days; but I will trust in thee." Some men will not live out half their days. Does that mean they will die an early death or does it refer to the quality of life some men will enjoy? I'm not sure we can truly say it refers to an early physical death. But clearly, the scriptures support death to the individual who rejects God in the next life, the second part of life yet to come. The Bible reveals to us that to reject Jesus is to forfeit heaven and embrace troubles without peace, despair without hope, and life that has torment as its end instead of eternal joy. The second half of life, the good half, is removed from one's grasp by refusing to receive Jesus as Savior and Lord of our lives.

COMPELLED TO RUN

e have all been compelled to run this race called "life." Life, however, is a lot longer than twenty-six miles, and it lasts more than one morning. Like the marathon run, life will require training and endurance to make it to the finish. At one time Rob could identify with those who say, "I don't want to run. I'd rather not get all worked up about it." Comments like, "I didn't choose this life," or "I did not choose to live here in this place like this," or "Why has all of this been thrust upon me?" Those statements may be true. But we are here, and we are alive. We may as well take the opportunity to get the most we can out of every day even though we did not ask to be here. We may not particularly like what life has dealt to us. All the more reason we should take advantage of the opportunities that lay before us. We should strive for a better future. A better future will be found when we are in fellowship with God.

But is a three letter word that changes everything it is associated with. The Bible is full of *buts*. In 1 Samuel 17:45-49 (KJV), the giant named Goliath intimidated the entire army of Israel, *but*! God sent a young man named David, who chose faith above fear. The giant came against David with a spear and sword, *but*! David stood on God's Word, killing the giant with a stone. In John 11:1-44 (KJV), the man Lazarus died and was buried, *but*! Jesus, the Resurrection, spoke life, and Lazarus rose from the grave. And John 8:1-11 (KJV), There was a woman accused of adultery, an act worthy of death by stoning, *but*! Jesus forgave and she was set free. Then in Mark 5:25-34 (KJV), there was another woman with an issue of blood that for twelve years doctors could not help her. She spent all the money she had and was not healed, *but*! She reached out one day and touched Jesus. Did you catch that? Many times Scripture shows God showing up at the right time, and that is always true. God is always there and never late, *but* this woman did not wait for God to come to her. She went after Him and reached out for her healing. Do you need a real change in your life? Reach out now to the only One that can change your life for the better. Running through life with God may not necessarily change the course or the obstacles along the way, *but*! One thing is guaranteed. When running through life with God, you will have the strength to overcome the obstacles and finish well while those running alone fail.

The thought of finishing the course of life well appeals to most everyone. To do so, we need to overcome the stumbling blocks that hinder us. Developing a strong, overcoming spirit is essential. *Develop is used here* because for many of us, we were not naturally born overcomers. It is a trait we can be taught and must learn and then continue to cultivate. People who never develop a get-over-it-attitude are at the mercy of every mishap in life. Happiness, joy, and success seem only for others. If care is not taken, anger, resentment, and jealousy become the nature of those who cannot forgive and move on. Teflon pans have held their popularity because food cooked in these pans is not supposed to stick. It is good for us to adopt the nature of not letting troubles stick to us and build up negative characters.

Everybody needs encouragement at times to overcome the obstacles encountered in life. Constantly building each other up and developing an overcoming spirit always works for good. We need to strive to have an "I can do all things through Christ" (Philippians 4:13, KJV) spirit about us all the time. We can start by surrounding ourselves with positive, overcoming, and encouraging people who speak and worship in a victorious manner. We should take care to start each moment of our day on a positive note. The last moment may have been a disaster, a fit of anger, a moment of fear, or a period of depression, *but* the next can be an upward, forward movement, toward a better life. What we do with the next moment will determine the outcome.

The book of Genesis records that the patriarch Jacob had a son with an overcoming spirit whose name was

Gad. Gad the son of Jacob would pass this character on down through his sons, who eventually became the tribe of Gad in Israel. The Hebrew language is said to have at least two meanings for every word. The word *Gad* follows this tradition, being interpreted "a troop cometh" or "good fortune." To get full understanding of why Leah named this son Gad, we should start in Genesis chapter 29. By looking at life through Leah's eyes, we can see the reason she chose the name Gad.

Leah began her marriage to Jacob in deception. On Jacob's wedding night, Jacob believed he was marrying Rachel, the woman he had loved and labored seven years for. Jacob and Rachel had spent days in excitement as the day of marriage approached. The night was set to seal the marriage. But Laban, Rachel's father, placed her sister Leah in the marriage tent that night instead of Rachel. Oh the troubles that would come to light in the morning. Jacob expected Rachel, but it was Leah who slept with him that night. Leah said nothing to inform Jacob of the deception. The next morning all the difficulties one can imagine in a marriage began for Jacob. He somehow took the wrong woman. Rachel, under authority and tradition, could say nothing of her father's decision in giving her sister to the man she loved. Rachel must have been furious. Leah realized quickly that spending a night with a man did not manifest the love she was desperate to receive. To say this was a mess is a vast understatement. Laban and Jacob tried to fix the situation by marrying Rachel to Jacob seven days later. This only doubled the troubles of Jacob. Jacob now had two wives, each fighting with one another for time and affection from him. This turmoil naturally spilled over into the lives of their sons as each was born.

Leah conceived first and bore a son. She named him Rueben. Notice what she said in Genesis 29:32 (KJV). "Surely the Lord has looked on my affliction; now my husband will love me." Leah felt afflicted. This feeling is at least partly her fault. Rueben's name means "see a son." You can almost hear Leah taunting Rachel. Leah's boast of producing a son while Rachel remained barren must have stirred the trouble between them even more.

The taunting probably escalated when Leah conceived again and gave birth to another son. This son she named Simeon, which means "God hears." By the time of Simeon's birth, she felt hated. Then came a third son, whom she named Levi, meaning "jointed to" or "added to." Leah was developing an attitude of hope. She had the feeling that Jacob would now love her because of the sons she had borne him. Leah was slowly gaining momentum. The score was Leah at three sons provided and Rachel still at zero. She gave birth to a fourth son she called Judah, whose name means "Now, I will praise."

In the circumstances of each birth, we can see a different character in Leah. First she felt afflicted, followed by feelings of being hated, and then by the time of Levi, she felt like she had something better in her life. By the time Judah arrived, Jacob must have been giving some attention toward Leah. He was by now training the boys in the methods of herding the flocks. Leah was busy now and had no time for self-pity. Her hands and heart were now praising God for the four boys that had brought Jacob's attention to her tent. Her attitude and character were now of praise. The names she chose for each son at birth reveal Leah's attitude changing for the better. Her change is revealed in the life and behavior of each son, as well. Isn't it interesting that the parent's attitude and characters show up in their siblings?

For a season after Judah, Leah provided no additional children. That was, until Rachel came up with the ingenious idea of giving Jacob children through her handmaid Bilhah. This idea proved to give Jacob two sons from Rachel, but the procedure did not heal the wounds in Rachel's life.

However, for Leah, this idea opened up an exciting new way to keep Jacob's attention. Why, the number of sons she could give Jacob through handmaids was virtually endless. What good fortune had come her way! By this method, a troop literally could come forth. She was excited and named the first son born through her handmaid Zilpah, Gad.

As said before, Gad in Hebrew means "a troop comes" or "good fortune." The best interpretation is found in the spiritual attitude of Leah, that is "there is more to follow." Imagine being called a name that constantly reminds you to expect more out of life. What a change in Leah's life! She surely found hope in the midst of her frustrations. Contrary to her old nature, Leah had developed a positive outlook in life. Now she chose a name that built, encouraged, and gave hope. It is always a pleasant surprise to find someone giving a word of encouragement. This change in Leah's life caused her to see how very fortunate she was and compelled her to name this son "good fortune." Joy and a new outlook continued to literally spill out of Leah as she named Gad "good fortune" and the son to follow him was Asher, which means "happy am I." Leah simply could not hide the joy that was filling her heart. I'm sure that every part of her life was now filled with excitement and expectation. The name Gad was surly a message to Jacob that if sons were what he wanted, he would soon have his own army of sons. Leah's choice of the name Gad became a point of constant encouragement to her and others. The new spirit that emerged in Leah developed into a ministry for others to expect more, expect more to follow, or something better was about to happen. Having a spirit of expectancy surely boosted everyone's morale. Boosted morale becomes infectious to those around. After years of bickering between the two wives, one can imagine the positive change in the dispositions of both wives as they gave children to the man they loved. Without a doubt, this joy spilled over into the lives of the entire family. This was life almost without limits. For everyone this was a great improvement over the past. Expectancy is the place where we give birth to almost everything we receive in life.

The colonel's invite was filled with expectancy. He could see an Army team competing in this event. He expected everyone to get excited about it, and he did his part as an excited leader. He did his best to give sound instructions on the art of running. He had run marathons before, so he had knowledge of what it took to prepare and accomplish the task. He did not come to the team meeting with an attitude of defeat, nor did he expect anyone to drop out. Some did drop, but he was sure to encourage them to try again. He did his best to develop the vision again in each person.

Expecting nothing usually gets you nothing, but expectation of something good to come normally produces something good. God has good things waiting for us. Are we willing to look forward to a better day; are we willing to expect a better way of life? Expectations of what the Lord can do will require faith—faith being something we hope for but right now it is not seen physically. This kind of faith will be developed by hearing God's voice, and the ability to hear His voice will come through the Word of God. Before reading next time, ask God to reveal how the passage applies to life. What thoughts come to mind as each verse is read? Read each word expecting God to speak to us through it. At first it may not seem like much, but as we continue, we will be building faith. Faith in God will produce visions that are heard and seen in the heart long before they are seen physically.

Faith that produces life and a change in life is typically developed in steps. First one step; then another builds upon that first step—then another until the goal is accomplished. The first step of faith anyone must make in a really successful life is receiving the saving grace that Jesus extended. Oh, sure, He died for everyone. But have we recognized He died especially for us? Can we see and receive the work on the cross He accomplished in order to give us abundant life here and eternal life in heaven? Sin separates us from living a life with God in heaven, and sin also disrupts the day-to-day blessings of God here in this life.

In the Old Testament, God revealed a method to remove sin. It included taking the life of innocent animals and offering their life and blood as a substitute sacrifice. Through this substitute, sin was removed from the one who made the offering onto the animal sacrificed. God promised that one day a redeemer would be provided, and these sacrifices would no longer be needed. This redeemer would be greater than all animal sacrifices ever given. That Redeemer was and is Jesus the Christ, the Son of God. He came to us in the flesh and lived a sinless life. His life and then the shedding of His blood on the cross is the only sufficient method of removing sin from our life. Now, we don't crucify Him again to accomplish the removal of sin. Instead we believe by faith that our sin was laid on Jesus. Jesus carrying our sin to the cross was enough sacrifice for all sin, for all time.

The question arises here as to how Jesus could carry my sin to the cross if I was not yet born to commit the sin. The answer is that God, who can see all of our life from before we are born, through present time, and beyond, foreknew all the sin we would commit. He collected sin from the beginning of man historically and all sin from the future This being collected, he laid this burden on His Son, Jesus. Jesus, a perfect man physically and spiritually, He alone was capable of carrying all sin past, present and future to the cross.

His blood spilt then still cleanses all our sin today. To receive this blessing of having our sin removed so that our souls appear clean before God, we speak a prayer in faith. Through prayer we acknowledge our desire for our sin to be included in the work Jesus did on the cross. By doing so the Holy Spirit steps in and removes the burden of sin from our soul and establishes His presence in our life. By faith we believe His life, death, and blood paid the price to remove all our sin. Faith allows us to see that His work on the cross long ago is for us today. That act of God's love toward us inspires us to live differently.

We are not saved by what we do; instead, we are saved by who and what we place our faith in. What saves us is the blood of Jesus. Who saves us is Jesus, God's Son. It is so important that I must say that again. You and I are saved by the shed blood of Jesus. The knowledge of this challenges us to begin living differently because we see what our Creator has done for us. We also see very quickly that He has called us to a different standard of living. He births in us a vision of living beyond the norm of everyday life.

Jesus is calling to each of us to come and run the race of life with Him. If you have never committed your life to Jesus, now is a great time. Take a moment to pray a short but powerful prayer. Pray something like this in your own words or use these printed here.

Pray, "Lord, I have sinned. I ask that you forgive me of all my sins against you Lord and other individuals. I believe Jesus died on the cross to pay the price of my wrong doings. I now believe His shed blood is a sufficient sacrifice to remove my sin. I ask you to direct my life and use me for your glory. I will begin to read your Word and speak with you daily to increase my faith. Help me, Lord, as I follow you. In Jesus's name, amen"

Hard Work and Vision

*C*hief Rob recognized that in order to run the marathon, he would need a great deal of help. On the day of the colonel's invite, he was not physically in shape to run five miles, let alone twenty-six miles. Rob felt he would require more than the standard exercise program. He needed nothing short of a miracle. He had started exercise plans before and had given up each time before accomplishing the set goals. Rob breathed a prayer, seeking the Lord for His wisdom and strength. God quickly began answering his prayer through a sermon preached in the church he attended. Without Rob telling the pastor anything about the run, the pastor ministered a message to the church on how the prophet Elijah ran twenty-five miles ahead of King Ahab. He spoke briefly of how God enabled the prophet to run that distance. God now had Rob's attention; he hung on every word spoken. In his mind he could almost see himself and the prophet running ahead of the king's chariot. Rob realized that

God knew his thoughts and was encouraging him by sending this message through the pastor. Rob began thinking that if God helped the prophet, he could receive help as well. *Lord knows,* Rob thought, *I need a lot of divine help in so many areas of my life.*

Each day he began by praying for the Lord to help him in the training. Rob entered a daily Bible reading program, spending time every day searching for the strength of the Lord. The Lord assured Rob in his spirit that he could do this run. Oh sure, it started small, and Rob began a little doubtful, but God showed Himself faithful, as He always does. Rob started first by running two miles and building his strength up so that one day he ran five miles; then he progressed to ten and on to twenty miles. On many days what started out as a run ended up in a walk, but Rob kept at it every day.

The Lord was consistently gracious and encouraging, often reminding him of where he started and how much had been accomplished since then. Sure it was tough to run these distances, but with God's help, it was happening. The Lord continually helped Rob by using people around him. Scripture verses he read each day seemed to be written just for him. The vision of accomplishing this goal grew along with his commitment to it. All Rob had to do was place one foot in front of the other—literally!

Training for the run took a lot of time. Rob quickly found out that he needed to schedule time for the things he deemed important. At this point, Habakkuk 2:2-3 began to make sense. It says,

And the LORD answered me, and said, write the
vision, and make it plain upon tables, that he
may run that readeth it. For the vision is yet for
an appointed time, but at the end it shall speak,
and not lie: though it tarry, wait for it; because
it will surely come.

Habakkuk 2:2-3, KJV

The vision will become a reality. Rob took that
advice and began by writing his overall goal. The big
picture was to run the Marine Corp twenty-six mile
marathon in Washington, DC. He did not want to
lose sight of what he started out to do. He wrote it
on everything. He even doodled it on the pages of the
phone book. Next Rob incorporated a system that he
called "mile stoning." This method is where he began
at the finish and systematically worked backward,
setting smaller or shorter yet reasonable goals that
were to be obtained before stepping up to the next
level. For example, in order to run twenty-six miles
the first week of November, he had to be able to run
at the very least twenty miles two times the month
prior to the marathon week. Before accomplishing
twenty, he must be able to run the distance of eighteen
miles twice in the month of September. Long runs, or
progress runs, were set for Saturday mornings when
he felt fresh and could accomplish the task without
interruptions. It took time to lay his plan out on the
calendar, but he reasoned that any adventure worth
undertaking would be worth the investment. As the
monthly progress runs increased in distance, so did the

weekly training schedule of total of miles to be run each week.

After the big goal schedule was finished, Rob got busy establishing smaller and more easily obtainable goals for each week. Running every day would become tiresome, and Rob thought his muscles might need a break to rest from the rigorous schedule. So he decided to run short, medium, and long runs to keep change in the amount of strain he placed on himself. Rob involved different exercises on two days to build his upper body. Rob's estimate for miles required per week for the last three weeks before the race was seventy miles. The daily schedule of miles to be run had to be flexible. Rob wanted family and church events to take place along with running. So some days were purposely scheduled to run short. Other days were longer depending on the required total for the week. By doing this, important events were scheduled in so he would not miss doing his responsibilities and the things he loved to do.

A daily plan written down kept Rob in focus with the vision and overall goal he had set. This plan gave Rob shorter goals that kept him encouraged. Physically seeing different levels accomplished toward the main event was rewarding. Having a plan helped prevent Rob from casting off all restraints and ignoring his family, church, or the training.

Mile stoning our vision is one method of helping us stay on track. It is a chart that is easy to read and should contain short goals that are quickly attainable. This will help us from casting off the restraint Proverbs 29:18 talks about. Casting off restraint is simply losing the desire to stick with the plan. People perish when they lose the desire to follow God's plan. Line of sight is very important here. Line of sight is the ability to see something constantly without any obstructions hindering our vision. Anytime we lose the line of sight, we are in danger of letting something else creep in and grab our attention. This is one of the devil's best work descriptions—stealing and destroying our vision of who we are in Christ Jesus. Writing the vision and having it posted in a highly visible location will help in maintaining direction toward the goal. Placing copies of our goals at home, in the office, in the car, and on daily planners will help keep us inspired. Everyplace we go we are kept in tune with our goals for running or any other activity.

Just writing a list of these things will not magically bring them into your life. Wanting something from the department store is one thing, but desiring a life change for yourself and others is very different. You have to approach it differently. Most times doing something big will require a great deal of input on your behalf. Oh, yes, there are times when God gives a vision and all you need to do is just stand still and watch it happen. But more common are the visions that require hard work. These visions energize our spirits and we are compelled to work toward what we see. We are told to write them down and make a plan. Then follow that plan to see it manifested. Too often we are guilty of wishing the dream would come true. We can be guilty of wanting to pass straight to the finished product with no investment in the process. Without proper planning and hard work, our dream may not be realized.

There never seems to be enough time to do everything we desire. Planning will help us not to take on too much at one time, where we may exhaust ourselves then everything becomes discouraging. Discouragement will cause us to dwell on the negative aspects. Dwelling on the negative will make it harder to do even the smallest task.

Rob began to rethink how he was going to accomplish everything he held valuable. First was to identify time-consuming activities that took away from what was most important. Second he chose the activities that worked toward his overall goals in life. Then he got rid of or limited all the rest. For Rob, TV was a real time consumer. He placed it at the top of a list of things that had to go. TV consumed too much time and produced no real benefits for the future. Rob decided that every activity had to somehow support his goals for family, church, and running. If the activity did not work toward improving these three, it was set aside.

Another real battle for Rob was that in the beginning he did not feel like a runner. He was not in physical condition to run very far. So he felt like the ability to run any great distance was never going to happen. Mile stoning the distances on a chart enabled him to see progress. It took time but after a few short running events, he began to see himself as a runner of *at least short distances*. This was important because Rob needed to *believe* he was a runner to *be* a runner. He was not going to *become* a runner. He *was* a runner! Running became a part of his character. Sure, he had a long way to go and much to learn in the world of running, but he was a runner. In short, Rob had to begin believing in himself.

Once we pray to receive Jesus as our Savior, we are a child of God. All the blessings and privileges of being in the family of God are ours. We don't need to wait any longer to be worthy of God's blessings. We are as much of a child of God as we will ever be. We can and are expected to grow in maturity, but we don't need to re-qualify as a child of God. We are His child. Maturing in Christ is an expected duty for all of us. Our desires should change toward everything in life. And our behavior patterns should begin to line up with what God has placed in His Word. Learning to pray effectively, entering into worship, and developing a Bible study plan all help us mature. Meeting with other believers, developing a sincere reverence for God and living a life that emulates Jesus will help us also. These are just a few areas we can direct our efforts in our quest to mature before the Lord. Along the way the Lord will use others to bless us, and He will use us to bless others. Changes will begin in how we walk out our life because of our relationship with Jesus. Evidence of our salvation will be revealed in the desire and willingness to change.

Changing our character and attitude into one that desires to do good things and give rather than receive will only occur after we begin to see things differently. Looking at life through God's eyes will change everything. God sent His Son to set us free from sin and to empower us to live our lives differently. Being set free from sin is one thing, the idea that He also wants to give us abundant life is another. A saved person with a defeated mindset is not the goal God set for us. Salvation is a starting point, because we cannot live victoriously without Jesus. God did not make Jesus the only way into heaven just so He could put us in our place and keep us in some sort of oppression. No, the entire plan of Calvary was to empower us with the ability to live life victoriously. Without salvation a victorious walk with God is impossible. The Father and Son's work of Calvary is the power point to overcome death and all the obstacles in life. Salvation opens up to us an entirely new way of viewing life.

How we see God's work and Word will determine what we will do with our lives. An example would be the Ten Commandments given by God and recorded for us by Moses. On that list is the commandment, "Thou shall not kill" (Exodus 20:13, KJV). Great idea! This commandment has been a blessing to all of us. However, the command at first appears controlling by stating you cannot do something. As we continue to mature in the Lord through Bible study and worship, we should see a change in how we live with this commandment. God's desire for you is not limited to living life without hurting one another. He has equipped us to give life. If all we see are the *thou shall nots*, we have seriously limited what God has set us free to do. We should not feel forced to live within the law of not killing. Instead, we should see in our spirit the awesome privilege of giving someone else a more abundant life. Helping others to have a better life can be done in countless ways. Our imagination is our only limitation. We must begin thinking deeper than what we cannot do and see all that we can. The vision God has for us is greater than getting stuff for ourselves. God is ready to give us the privilege of enhancing life for others. Plus God will honor His word of not muzzling the ox. We will be blessed in our being a blessing. Living through the years without killing one another sounds good but it also has a ring of selfishness. God's calling for each of us is to enhance life for those who are in need. Life is not about the *shall nots*. Instead, real life is about helping others gain a better life because Christ is in us. He will supply and strengthen those who are doing something to honor Him.

Imagine if all the resources in the world were at our disposal. If we could do anything we wanted to that gave honor to God, what would it be? Search the scriptures and spend some time in prayer. Will the idea honor the Lord? Yes, then take a step. Give the vision to the Lord and let Him lead. God will provide the resources needed especially if the endeavor is to help others grow closer to Him.

Is the vision worth our labor? That is a tough question we must ask ourselves. There are hundreds of ideas that are easy to talk about. But when it comes to getting involved, the ideas become an entirely different matter. This idea that we have, is it more important than the next moment of pleasure? We may think someone else is better qualified to perform the task, but the Lord apparently did not see it that way. He chose us! That is a great, big compliment coming from heaven. God thinks mighty highly of us! God chose to place the vision with us. Why? Because He knows we will let Him work through us. God is not interested in what we can do for Him. The Lord is more interested in those He can work through.

About the time Rob would think it was time to do a short run, the devil would remind him of a favorite television program or of another person who would be better at this endeavor would come to mind. There seemed to be no end to the excuses the devil could place in his mind. Battling with these thoughts all came to a head one day. He looked into the mirror and told his reflection, "God chose you, not the other guy."

There were some days Rob would realize he had not run the programmed miles for that day. He would then push himself into his shoes and go for a run to fulfill the task assigned for the day. While running, he would determine to get up earlier in the morning to put in the next day's mileage before the day stole his dream. Rob knew that after two or three days of not running, giving up the effort would be easy. Rob knew it was important to maintain his line of sight.

Faith is seeing in our spirit what is not yet there and knowing it will soon appear (Hebrews 11:1, KJV). God has a plan for us to live a full and vibrant life that honors Him. He has sent His Son that we might have life and that life is to be abundant (John 10:10, KJV). When Jesus ascended to heaven, He sent the Holy Spirit to reveal what God has for us through His written Word and through visions and dreams.

God promised to give visions to His followers. Visions are a vital part of looking forward to each day. Vision gives hope and the ability to cope with everyday trials and tribulations. When people are without a vision of *hope*, they begin to perish. They die from despair. The lack of having a reason to go on is devastating. To those who lose hope, there seems to be no reason to go forward. There are visions that come from the Lord, and there are visions that come from people. Both may give a spark of hope, but only a vision from God can produce life. This is why it is important to read the Scriptures every day. Reading will build our faith, and faith produces vision of how we can be involved in building the Kingdom of God.

An interesting thing about vision is that we all have the ability to cast vision into the life of others. Most parents cast vision in their children without realizing it is happening. Our outlook on life, the way we interpret the surroundings we live in, is generally picked up from our family members. Everyday prejudices are passed down from generation to generation through the daily conversations in the home. An older person may reflect on the way something appeared to them, and, unwittingly, the child picks up this idea as truth for his or her life. Studying people's habits and character allows us to see that the mindsets of the parents are often revealed with greater intensity in the children. So it is very important that we choose a good vision and example to live by because it will mold our children as well as our future. Much of the racial and religious beliefs we have were passed down by our family members. When these beliefs are challenged, we may have trouble finding where they originated. It may appear as though these beliefs have always been with us. The Lord's desire for us is that we adopt His view of life and His method of behavior. These patterns for living are found in the Scriptures.

Rob laughed at himself over an account that fits into this category. Before he received salvation, he watched a movie titled *The Ten Commandments*. After salvation he read through the biblical account of the Ten Commandments and thought, *That's not correct. In the movie it said...* It took a moment to realize that the Bible was correct, not the movie. He had to challenge where he received this information and whether it was truth. There were many other beliefs he had to challenge as he began to study the Bible. The principles we have been taught or picked up on over the years, are they really biblical? It may be hard to change our way of thinking, but the Lord is there to constantly support us. God and His Word are always absolute truth.

Jacob fathered twelve sons, whose families grew and became the tribes in the nation of Israel. Jacob's sons and Israel's tribes walked out the character that the parents had at the time of their birth. Some changed, but not all. Gad was born seventh to Jacob and Leah through the handmaid Zilpah. It appears Gad was an average boy with no physical talent that would cause him to be exalted above his brothers. He did have one outstanding quality that was revealed throughout his life and the tribe he fathered: he was an overcomer. Regardless of the order of our birth or the circumstances in which it might have occurred, we have the same opportunities as anyone else. The behavior pattern we choose will determine much of the success we will enjoy. The difference in our lives will be the vision we cling to and walk by as we move toward our future.

There are hundreds of books that tell the stories of men and women who have beaten unbelievable odds. They all somehow include the individual's vision, hope, or determination of having a better life. One key to success is to fight off discouragement. Countless times we have all been told to never give up. If something goes wrong in an endeavor, don't throw in the towel. Instead look at the situation again. Find out why it didn't work. Determine what will work and do it again until success is realized. Advice from successful people as to how they made it usually has the same formula. The major keys to their successes were maintaining vision and never giving up. The main reason people can overcome setbacks along the way is that in their mind's eye, in their spirit, they can still see the goal. Their eye is searching for the goal rather than the problems. Problems become stepping stones toward the goal. The vision of the goal is not erased by a difficult time. Instead, difficulties conjure up a hidden emotion that lies deep inside of the heart that says, "Oh, I should have expected that. Why, I'll just change this or that and see how it turns out." Or if it's a serious setback, there's a determined emotion that announces, "I will not be defeated by this!" Keeping one's eye on the goal spurs one on to do what has not yet been tried or to try again what they feel in their heart will work. There are some things in life that we just know God gave to us. These ideas or dreams become rooted deep in our spirit. We may not know how it is going to happen, but there's an assurance it will. We should also know that no one or no circumstance can take it away, because it belongs to us. Life with God, abundant life, should be one of those things. Our life is ours! Get a vision of how God desires us to live it. Then *run* in that vision!

The story of Jesus walking on the water is recorded in Matthew 14:22-33. One stormy evening, the disciples were traveling in a boat when they saw Jesus walking on the water. Peter called out to Him, "Lord if it be you bid me come unto thee on the water." Jesus did call Peter, saying, "Come." Peter instantly moved toward the Lord without thought of walking on the water. Then we read that Peter saw the waves and began to sink into the water he was walking on. Praise the Lord, it is good to note that Jesus did not sink with him. Jesus never lost sight of what He was called to do. If Peter would have only kept his eye on the goal, he would not have sunk into the very substance he was called to walk on as well. We miss a great lesson here in the story if we stop at the point of only seeing Peter's failure. Ever wondered how Peter got back to the boat? The answer is the Lord took hold of him, and Peter walked back to the boat just like he walked out on the water. Just because we failed once that doesn't mean the walk is over. Let the Lord take hold, and walk again.

Sometimes our activities don't produce results that line up with our vision. In order to obtain a different outcome, we will have to change what we do. For many, change can be scary. We get comfortable with our situations regardless of how harsh they might be. We have a want or a desire to have a different life but hesitate to change anything due to fear of the unknown. Conforming to a new way of life can be scary. What if it doesn't work? But what if it does? Then it is worth the efforts of change! Fear can be a stumbling block to following a vision. Fear is the opposite of faith, faith being from God verses fear being from the devil. Faith is the ability to see a vision and trust God will help us get there. Fear is lack of trust; we still see the vision, but we also see and entertain reasons the vision won't work. Entertaining the reasons it won't work reduces our vision to a wish with no work toward the vision. We wish it would happen, but... We then become disappointed when our wishes don't produce the results we hoped for. Trying to overcome life's obstacles with wishes or using our own strength can be extremely fearful and difficult. It could be time to employ outside help. God can make a difference. Regardless of the level on which we may know Him, He is interested in our life. His perfect love toward us and our developing a love for Him will cause fear to leave and faith to develop. Understanding that God desires to work through each of us, using His abilities, not ours, dispels a lot of fear. Having the knowledge that God is on our side is empowering. God does want us to succeed! The Lord is glorified when we do well and acknowledge it was His blessings, and His power, that allows for our successes.

Imagine our car out of fuel in the country filled with valleys and hills. Pushing the car along the highway up the hills and across valleys would be tremendously difficult. It would be a lot easier if the fuel tank was filled with the proper propellant. Life is the same. To move through life victoriously, we will need to fill our life with the correct propellant. A vision of who we are with and in the Lord Jesus the Christ will help us. His presence will enable us to climb every mountain and pass through every valley with power and control. It could be we have had a tough start. Don't let this stop us from making the next decision correctly. Take a moment to pray the most powerful prayer in life. Ready? Pray aloud. *Jesus, help us in this...I need you.* Amen. Now begin to thank Him for His answer. Praise Him until He answers ; then give Him praise for His answer. Don't get discouraged; keep thinking positive. He has heard, and He will answer. Sometimes He may answer yes or no instantly. Other times the answer may be delayed. Be assured He is interested in us and the events in our life. He will be dispatching angels to come to our aid. How will we know His direction for us? Read His Word, God often confirms our prayers through the Bible. He never contradicts His own written promises. Listen to Holy Spirit-filled people; they may lead us toward His answer. Find a positive, encouraging church that speaks the truth of Scripture so that we may learn and prosper in our spirit. All Jesus expected of Peter was that he would come unto Him. All Jesus asks is that we would be willing to come. Fix your attention upon Jesus. Begin to walk toward Him. Determine to know His voice and character. Start moving. Look expectantly as you run the race of life toward the author life.

BLESSED IS HE THAT ENLARGES ANOTHER

$\mathcal{M}$oses gave a special word to the tribe of Gad just before he died. "Blessed is He that enlarges Gad" (Deuteronomy 33:20, KJV). Moses, speaking those words, reminded the tribe of Gad and everyone else that all good gifts come from the Lord. It is not hard to figure out that God is in the blessing business. He blesses those who will believe in His Son who hung on the cross. He blesses us by providing our daily provisions. He blesses us with His Word that encourages all who read it daily. His Word indicates we are made in His image. From there we should determine to live our life emulating His life, by being a blessing to others.

One thing that Rob came to appreciate was the team meetings where each runner shared the ups and downs of training. Conversations of finishing the marathon and how they would celebrate afterward became a big part of each meeting. Each runner was building a vision of finishing the race well, and oddly enough, these visions included one another together. It was not long and every member on the team began telling of longer distance runs and obstacles that were overcome in their exercise times. Success was in their hearts, and it became contagious. The group began to express joy and encouragement toward one another. Those positive times helped build hope in the runners who were struggling with their training.

So often we will find people who dwell on the negative aspects of life, always talking about the down side of any situation. People who can only see what won't work or think about what cannot be done usually don't accomplish much. These people are dangerous to maintaining a positive attitude, and we should do our best to limit how much time we spend listening to their negative speech. We should surround ourselves with friends that are willing and able to encourage. Encouraging words build; *negative* words destroy.

As we seek out places and people that will help in reaching our goals, we should also take opportunity to encourage others. We will find sowing and reaping very rewarding. It is absolutely amazing how great it feels when people come back and give us credit for being there in their hour of need. Truly, it is a blessing to enlarge another. "Blessed be he that enlargeth Gad" (Deuteronomy 33:20, KJV). Moses was talking of the Lord I am, sure, but the principle applies to us as well. Blessings will follow those who encourage others.

Overcoming-type people understand that doing something for someone else always has rewards. Overcomers are not afraid to give thanks to those who have helped them get to where they are. It usually costs nothing physically to give an encouraging word to those around you, and it surely costs nothing to give God praise for the great things He does for us each day. Moses encouraged Israel. Jesus encouraged the disciples. Scripture encourages us. Shouldn't we build and encourage others?

"Sticks and stones may break my bones, but names can never hurt me." That's part of a rhyme repeated often, but it simply is not true. Those prone to degrading speech and name calling should stop! How shall a Christian minister the love of God after cursing or negative, degrading speech has come out of his or her mouth? The Scripture asks in James 3:11 (KJV), "Can a fountain produce both good and bitter water from the same faucet? The answer is no, it cannot. The fountain is one or the other. Our speech should be consistent. Telling a dirty joke one moment and speaking of how much we love the Lord the next sends a very confused message to the listener. God's children do not speak this way. This also reveals a lack of love for the Lord. Either we are followers of Christ, or we are not. We are admonished by the apostle Paul to encourage and build lives in Romans 14:19. It is sad to think so few saints have stepped up to perform this valuable ministry. Words have the ability to cut deeper than knives, and the damaging effect can last well past the physical pain of being beaten with a stick. One of the greatest gifts God has given each of us is the ability to build hope in the lives of those who have lost hope. To do this great work, we will have to use our tongue. Christians should be known for their attitude and counsel of "I can do all things through Christ; all things are possible to those that believe" (Philippians 4:13; Mark 9:23). Negative, degrading speech is something we stand against. We are to be the *light*, not the night, of the world.

Having a name like Gad meant being called "a troop," "good fortune," or "more to follow" each day of his life. More to Follow, take out the trash. More to Follow, do this or do that. His name was a constant reminder of something more to follow. Now the one called to take out the trash, may not want to hear that there will be more. But if there is to be more trash, then that also indicates more of something good was consumed. Why else would there be trash lest the good had been consumed ? How we view things will determine greatly how we are able to handle difficult times and how much we will be able to enjoy everyday life. Names meant more in those days than just a label. One's name may have described a significant event in their life or their character and maybe even the character of God. To hear one's name was a message of who they were or what they represented. When others hear our name, who or what character do they associate it with?

Rob's life has been very similar to Gad. He grew up with seven other siblings. Due to the large number in his family, it was common to hear comments like, "The

Robinson tribe is here." Now, some would take offense to being referred to as a tribe or troop. Rob's family did not mind being called a troop. Why? Because they knew they were large in number. Very often they would refer to themselves as a troop. Rob's family was large, and it was a challenge to entertain them, and some people were not strong enough to meet that task. Rob's parents taught that wherever they went, the boys were to be a blessing. Take out the trash, help with the dishes, or simply carry something for someone else or give up their seat. The boys grew up doing more than their part, and God always ensured a blessing for the efforts. Churches would rejoice when the Robinson tribe visited because they would fill up the entire pew. If anyone took on the challenge of feeding the family, that always was a noteworthy testimony.

Instead of living with the shame of negative remarks, it is safe to assume this young man Gad grew up with a sense of expectation of more to come. Gad was always ready to go when called upon, which was probably due to the sense of duty to do their part and the expectation of coming home with a reward. God always has more to give to those who expect more.

One day, a young boy named Timothy wanted ice cream from the roaming ice cream truck just like any other child in the area. Normally this cost much more than purchasing ice cream at the grocery store. His mom, being on a tight budget, did not buy ice cream from the roaming truck very often. She said to the young lad one day, "Let's ask God to bring us some." They prayed just that and left it in the Lord's hands.

She did that primarily because money was tight. The next day a semi truck carrying ice cream was involved in an accident on the highway. The dairy company decided to, rather than allow the ice cream to be lost to the heat of the summer day, donate the frozen delight to the local mission where Timothy's father worked. A driver from the mission arrived at the boy's house with a pickup truck loaded with ice cream, which was more than enough for the family and all the neighborhood children. All Timothy's friends were called to come quickly and enjoy a treat. Each child that came and sat at the picnic table with a half gallon of the ice cream. God rewarded a very expectant heart with so much he could share.

As a young adult, Rob joined a very popular men's organization that he came to realize later was a cult. Rob was searching for something more in life. He stood up one night in a meeting and stated his desire for more insight to life. He had received a promise on entering this fraternity that they took good men and made them better. His expectation of *better* was not met. He found the principles taught applied only to members of the fraternity and their families. Non-members did not deserve the same treatment. This limited arena of reform seemed shallow to him. His involvement with the fraternity started under a cloud of secrecy, and it was not fulfilling. As the years went by, Rob found out that most everything born in secret will not remain fulfilling. That is because it fails the biblical principle laid out in Habakkuk 2:2 of writing the vision openly and clearly so that anyone who desires to run may do so. Visions are to be spoken of and written down for all to see. Secrecy is not an element of a godly vision. God gives visions to be proclaimed and shared.

Scripture says openly that Gad was born to the handmaid. The fact of being born to the maid may be embarrassing. Most people would probably prefer to keep this a secret from the public. However, in Gad's life, nothing was hidden. His birth was not something kept in the dark. He knew his birth mother was Zilpah. He knew Leah commanded Zilpah to lie with Jacob for the sole purpose of breeding another son and then took him as her own. Everyone knew the stress between the wives. I am sure that, living close to one another in tents, no conversation or action was hidden from anyone. A wonderful thing about God is that He exposed everything—good *and* bad. At the same time, He revealed His position on each subject. Most everything we do in secret will have a negative effect on a person or a relationship. A good thing to remember is that if you cannot say or do something openly, you probably shouldn't do it at all.

Leah's marriage started in secret—deceiving Jacob on the wedding night. This deception caused her to feel hated and not loved. There was a cost to her negative thoughts and actions. Sure, as time went by, Leah's feelings and mindset changed. But her first-born son deceived his father by sleeping with one of his wives. This type of behavior and method of thinking started long before Rueben was born. Rueben held the same behavior pattern as did his mother, Leah, his grandmother, Rebekah, and his grandfather, Laban. We can see deception was entertained long before Rueben and followed the family through the generations.

By the time Gad was born, Leah's outlook on life and her disposition had improved greatly. She became a person of character, possessing a spirit of expectation, and as a result named her son accordingly. Gad's disposition became a reflection of Leah's attitude at the time of his birth. In fact, each of Jacob's sons held a disposition that was closely associated with the attitude of his two wives when the sons were born. Evidence of Leah's change was reflected in Gad's name and character. Leah had entered into a spirit of expecting something more.

There is a story of a woman preparing for her burial. She tells her pastor that her desire is to be buried with a fork in her hand. He thought this strange and asked why. The woman's reply was, "Life is just like a supper meal. After the dinner comes desert. It was always announced in our house to keep our fork because the best was yet to come." Life is offering more, and God is offering better. Don't quit now; our next choice will make a difference in our future. Hold on to the dream that life will get better. Remember, with Jesus, the best is yet to come!

A spirit of expectation should be about all of us because God rewards a positive, faith-filled person with more (Ecclesiastes 2:26, KJV). "Cast not away therefore your confidence, which hath great recompence of reward," (Hebrews 10:35, KJV). Also see Ruth 2:12, Proverbs 11:18, and Revelation 22:12 That alone is a good reason for each of us to live expectantly. Who knows what God will do next! Like David, you could be shepherding sheep one day, and through God's choosing, a king the next. God's blessing on Gad enabled him to become an overcomer. Our blessings toward others could be the key to developing other overcomers as well. Through Proverbs 18:21 and Galatians 6:1, God challenges us to speak differently by choosing positive words that build, heal, restore, and encourage others to walk with Him. We have been offered a great tool called *encouragement*. And we should use it to the best of our ability through Christ. Blessed will be the saint that builds another!

DIAMONDS HAVE INCREDIBLE VALUE

A diamond placed on a dark background shines brilliantly when light is present. The light reflecting through the diamond reveals hints of color and beauty. Because diamonds are rare, extremely hard, and posses this uncommon beauty, they have incredible value. Due to these rare qualities, people tend to spend a great amount of money to obtain them. In short, diamonds are valuable, and most everyone is attracted to them.

The position of the tribe of Gad on the Breastplate of the High Priest and the stone that represents him can be determined by searching just a few scriptures. The tribes of Israel are listed in Numbers chapter 2. Here they are divided into four groups consisting of three tribes in each group. Exodus 28:15-21 reveals that God directed Moses to place the stones in four rows with three stones in each row. By listing the stones in the order of Exodus 28 then placing the names in order as recorded in Numbers 2, the result is that the diamond stone represents the tribe of Gad.

All the stones including the diamond were inscribed with the name of each tribe before being placed on the breastplate. How did they inscribe the name of Gad in the diamond, you ask? Good question! Most of us have been taught that nothing scratches a diamond. So how did Israel write on the diamond stone? Actually, another diamond can cut a diamond. In Jeremiah 17:1 (KJV), it reveals Israel had knowledge of an iron pen with a diamond point. However, regardless of what method was used to write on the diamond, it was done. I find it very important to remember that our God created the universe, and He divided the Red Sea. He also stopped the Jordan River, and He raised the dead to life. We can be quite confident that He can write on a rock.

Gad's place on the breastplate was on the second row in the last position. He was in the middle of the twelve. We know he was born seventh in the line of sons, and here Gad the tribe holds position six on the breastplate of judgment.

It is important to note the breastplate is described as one of judgment. The question must be asked, what is being judged? Scripture clearly indicates that God is interested in our behavior. We are not to walk as the heathen nations walk. God has revealed a standard of living that He has called us to live above what is called normal. God is holy, and He has invited us to live as ambassadors for Him by living differently. Careful study of the names and behavior of the tribes of Israel will teach us much about how we should develop and conduct our lives.

Judgment surely indicates a decision between something, a rank and order, or a scale of not good, good, better, and best. Judgment could refer to a position of maturity, our growing up in the Lord. Our character is to improve as we grow in the wisdom and knowledge of the Lord. There is an expectation of change after we come to the Lord seeking forgiveness of our sin. Jesus told the woman in John 8:11 (KJV) to go and sin no more. He expected a change in her behavior. Yes, God forgives our sin. He also expects us not to continue doing the same sinful things.

The tribes' behavior traits and characteristics placed them on the breastplate in an order that reveals spiritual growth. It is not my desire to demean or cast negative light on any son or tribe of Israel. I am merely revealing that in each son's name, there is a character type that was passed down from the parent. There is also for all to see an expected growth pattern to learn from as they grew in maturity. The attitudes of Jacob's wives are revealed in the scriptures as they name each son. That attitude spilled over and became at least part of the character of each tribe as well. These traits were passed on by the women to each of their sons unknowingly and eventually became a part of the character of the tribes.

The same thing happens to people today. I'm sure that as soon as any parent realizes their own personal negative attitude is developing in a child, they are inclined to change quickly. Most parents want the very best for their children in material goods and behavior patterns. The possibility still exists that some parents did not recognize this, and their children may have picked up on some not-so-good personality qualities. This is not a license to say, "I behave badly because of my parents" and continue to do so. That simply does not have to be true. This may be breaking news for some people, but people act the way they do because they choose to. We think and act the way we do because that's who we believe we are or because of pressure from our peers. People who unite with the Lord will change their way of thinking and their behavior. If we behave wrongly, we can change when we want to. If we have no desire to change, we should examine our relationship with God. No desire to change could mean we have no relationship with God at all. No relationship means we will not be in heaven. True believers want change in their lives that will bring honor and glory to the Lord. Change may be hard coming, but real believers possess a burning desire that continually pushes them to strive for change. If we fail, we try again until we master the growth expected just as we expect our children to grow up and master their shortcomings.

Visualize for a moment the breastplate with four rows of stones with three stones in each row. Each stone is a different color and transparent in nature. Some stones were opaque, but for our illustration, we need light to shine through them. The various stones represent a character trait revealing behavior patterns and/or personal dispositions. These stones also have a different value and are placed in order one through twelve, with one being the top row first position. Our desire of course is to grow in maturity in each area until all twelve steps of maturity have been accomplished. Judah, the first stone, represents our highest calling and indicates one of the greatest levels of spiritual maturity. Judah, whose name means "praise," was placed first on the top row. Naphtali, placed last on the bottom row, represents the entry level or beginning struggles of wrestling against God's plan for our life. The object for each of us is not necessarily to move in order from bottom to top—though, that is acceptable—but rather to insure that we have the correct disposition in our character at all twelve stones.

If there were lights behind each stone that could be lit when developing the godly character spoken of in each position, our goal would be to have all twelve lights lit all the time as we walk through life. This is not a chart of working toward salvation. Instead, it is a belief and behavioral level that we strive to attain as we assume our position as ambassadors for the Lord after salvation. It is possible that we could have some lights lit midway up the plate and others dark. Dark or very dim lights would indicate areas that need improvement in our character. For sake of ease, I will refer to the chart as moving from bottom to top.

Consider each position, starting with Naphati at the bottom. In order to move on to the next block in spirit and truth, you must first conquer the preceding blocks. One will never be truly happy *Asher* if wrestling

Naphati against God. Just as you will not be truly blessed, *Ephraim,* until you can let go of yesterday, *Manasseh.*

The following chart will give us a picture of the breastplate of judgment with the names and short abbreviated note as to the meanings and character of each tribe.

Judah = praise, a spirit of giving God praise, all the time.	Issachar = burden bearer, the ability and willing to carry the burden for others	Zebulun = dweller, go proclaim the gospel to others everywhere
Ruben = stability, solid in Christ or unstable as water.	Simeon = God hears, listening to God or living for myself.	Gad = more to follow, living with an expectant spirit, overcomer.
Ephraim = doubly blessed, blessed here and going to be blessed there	Manasseh = forgetful of the past, moving toward the future	Benjamin = a son of the right hand, a true spiritual child of God
Dan = judgmental, holding up the truths of God or your own.	Asher = happy, happy content or happy and apathetic.	Naphtali = wrestling with God or against God.

Tribe order on the breastplate of the High Priest, each tribe in position according to Numbers 2. Below each tribe name is the name meaning with

a brief description of character type associated with
the tribe's name and their mothers' attitudes at the
times of their births.

The individual character type for each tribe begins
with the meaning of each of their names. The names
written on each stone represent the character traits
of the sons of Jacob. These character traits obtained
at the birth of each of Jacob's sons were passed down
to the tribe. The trait determined the location on the
breastplate. The direction of the movement of each
name from birth order to tribe order may be the greatest
indicator of character value. Some moved up from
their birth order, and others fell down, each according
to the character they developed and chose to live by,
praise being God's highest calling on all of creation
and wrestling with God or His directives being lowest.
How do we know praise is first? Philippians 2:10 (KJV)
says, "At the name of Jesus every knee should bow."
Every created being, every person who has ever been
given life, will praise Him. This applies to every soul,
both good and evil, whether in heaven or hell, and
it will include those who die before taking a breath
in life. Throughout Scripture God reprimands Israel
for not praising Him. Praise is our highest calling in
life! People who do not reach the level of praising God
will never reach their full potential in life. There are
some saints that have never told another soul of the
saving grace of Jesus. Yet the Bible says these people
who win souls are wise. Witnessing is a form of praise.
Many people have no desire to read God's Word. Yet

the Scriptures reveal God's will for our lives. Many of these great privileges will one day be gone, but the act of bowing our knees for praise and worship to God will be forever.

We should take a moment now and look at behavior and ask, what type of character do I have? Am I blessed and praising God or am I thinking critically and judgmentally of others? Our position might be different at different times in our spiritual walk. As we grow closer in our relationship to God, we will see change. As we mature in God's goals for us, we will think and behave the same on Monday and Tuesday as we do on Sunday. We will dispose of our Sunday-best behavior and walk in our Christ-like behavior twenty-four hours a day, seven days of the week.

God's choice of the diamond to represent Gad first speaks of hardness. A Gad-type person is steadfast in his walk in honoring God. He stood for God's standards to the best of his abilities, knowledge, past experiences, and instructions allowed him. He fixed his mind on serving God. Changing the diamond rock by cutting and polishing it is difficult. Leah took time to change her outlook of life. It was difficult to change old habits and let go of old ways of thinking. She was reformed under great pressure. Her change from the negative attitudes and deceitful practices to an honest and positive outlook must have been like a brilliant light shining in the family.

The diamond represented hard men who were tough and courageous. They were ready to overcome all obstacles and serve God with out fear, regardless of the cost. Gad men were like this. Gadites were not wishy-washy-type people, changing their minds every time the wind blew. Gadites did not change their beliefs just because the day was difficult. Vastly different from some of our leaders today that change sides according to votes and money. Gadite-type leaders were not in the habit of chasing money or fame. Deuteronomy 33:21 (KJV) states that Gad would meet with the leaders of the nation. He knew what they were supposed to believe and helped them stick to it. Biblical leaders that were great grew close to the Lord or they lost the position they held. Great leaders have convictions that run deep in their hearts. Gadites were tough people who were ready to fight for the Kingdom every time the King called. There was no hesitation when the leadership called for action. When called on to leave their own possessions and fight for the other tribes, they reported promptly. They took commands well from Moses, Joshua, and David. Our world would be in better shape today if we had a few more men of this type in our mist.

Ruben and Simeon were also very hard men. But their hardness was not in the correct areas. They too are represented by very hard stones, but they were not willing to change when God convicted them. Rueben and Simeon were born first and second and should have held their positions according to birth order and traditional law, but instead they fell to positions fourth and fifth on the breastplate. These two older brothers displayed a character that God judged to be lower than His top row. The position of the double blessing Ruben once held was given to another. Gad was born seventh, and he rose to position six on the breastplate. His ability to overcome life's stumbling blocks and stay positive is appealing. An overcomer's mindset is to live life with a get-over-the-past and believe-there-is-a-better-future attitude. It requires hope and faith. Gad's character and response to God's leading was positive.

Many saints today believe they can live any way they choose, and God will not be concerned. That is simply not true. God in His grace does take us just as we are at the point of our salvation. But He expects us to change, to conform to His way of thinking, His way of faith, and His way of living. After all, it is God's kingdom we are adopted into. Imagine you have adopted a child. How would you expect them to behave in your home? Think of the chaos it would be if we allowed the adopted child to live as they did when they were homeless or as they did if they came from the jungle. Each child cannot be in charge of what is right and wrong. Standards are set by the parent. Without the parent there would be no standard. It would be a world where everyone does according to their own heart. Hey, isn't that in Scripture? Did not our God judge people for this method of living? Our hearts and minds should be fixed on God and His Word. His Word, by the way, never changes. It is unchangeable. When God reveals sin or errors in our beliefs, we should be willing to change. Due to our hardness and reluctance to change, God allows trials and tribulations to bring our attention to areas in life that need change.

Changing our ways is difficult largely due to weakness in the knowledge of the Scriptures and lack of trust in the Lord's promises. Many are unable to discern the voice of the Holy Spirit due to sin-filled living. Many have justified their particular sin because of the pleasure it brings immediately rather than resist temptation and hold fast to the promises God gives for the future. Gad was no different. He often learned his best lessons the hard way. Just as diamonds increase their value when they are cut and polished, we as individual ambassadors for the Lord will increase our value through the cutting away of sin and the polishing of our hearts and minds to reflect Him. The most valuable people are those who can overcome difficulties and changes while maintaining direction and vision. These men and women move up in life and in purpose. We all know of certain habits we live with that do not honor God. Attempting to live halfway for God progressively gets more difficult. The difficulties keep increasing until we either draw closer to God for help or pull ourselves away from His presence due to conviction. Just as the tide on the sea comes closer and then pulls away, drawing with it particles of land, God through His Spirit does much the same. He draws near and encourages us then pulls back a little to see if we will follow. God wants us to follow Him closely in all ways all the time.

In Old Testament days, the best and safest part of the kingdom was inside the limits or walls of the established kingdom. To live on the outer fringes meant you were probably subjects of the kingdom to be taxed but too far away to enjoy kingdom benefits. To enjoy the best, one wanted to live close within the walls of the kingdom headquarters. How much difficulty can we take in life before we decide to move closer to the Lord for our own benefit?

Once we decide to really live for God, He begins to put us on display before others just like a jeweler places a precious jewel stone against a dark background. Dark backgrounds bring out the color and beauty of a diamond that might otherwise be overlooked. Our lives before coming to Jesus become dark, embarrassing backdrops. After deciding to follow Jesus, the light of God now shines through for others to see the great work God has done. As living stones, we are to glisten and sparkle like diamonds against life's darkness so that others who need Him can see His craftsmanship. When Peter called us "living stones," he was not referring to a dull, drab stone one finds in the drive way. No, he most likely was thinking of the beautifully cut stones that adorned the high priest's breastplate. What a privilege it is to be chosen by the almighty God and have Him shape and remold us into vessels of light. What an awesome opportunity we have. With darkness all around us, it is the perfect time to let God chip away the imperfections of our lives and reveal to the world what He can do with a life totally given over to Him.

In order to run the marathon, Rob had to change the way he lived and the way he thought. His weekend-couch-potato lifestyle had to come to an end. His eating habits had to change. Now he was in training, and it made a difference what he put into his body. The hours he slept and the activities he was involved in all had to go through a major transformation. Every part of his life had to support the endeavor he was undertaking. Rob began to think and live as a runner. He purchased running gear and studied running methods. He began searching out practices that would help him build his tomorrows. His exercise program had to build not only his legs but his arms and mind as well. It became a total fitness effort. All his being would be taxed before the race was over. The beginning days of training were difficult; change was fearsome.

Rob was not in shape physically. He was carrying a lot of extra weight. These pounds caused him to be very self-conscious of how others viewed him. But Rob had come to the decision point where he was going to do what was right for himself and ignore what others said. Sure, some mocked, but more importantly, many others were encouraged to live better and build stronger bodies. Rob's prayer was that his life would influence others positively. His hope was that others who might be struggling in some way would see how God helped him and know they too could have that help to change.

In the race of life, we need to be mindful of what we put into ourselves, what foods we eat, what shows we watch, what we read and where we go. Everything that we let into our lives will make a difference in how well we will run the course. In life, every part of our personal being will be tested and taxed to the very limits and sometimes beyond. Our mind will be stretched, our body will be flexed, and our emotions will be stirred during this run we call life. Many have said God will not give us more than we can handle. This is only true to those who are walking with the Lord. Life has a way of overloading people with more than they can handle alone. But with God, anything can be overcome. The Lord desires to help us with the simple things as well as the more complex struggles. Going to Him daily with the simple prepares us for the more difficult events. When faced with the stress that comes with illnesses, family issues, financial woes, or the loss of loved ones, many turn to substance abuse, seclusion, or worldly counselors. This will only mask the pain for a short period of time. All around us we see the stresses of life causing people to end their lives or the lives of others. God's Word quietly offers to everyone that He will carry our burdens should we be willing to change and live for Him. Life is a race of endurance that requires additional strength to overcome the stumbling blocks along the way, and we need help!

We need to start now in preparing and protecting ourselves. What we feed ourselves in secret will affect our abilities to run in public. Our diet must be made up of food that builds life. Elements that destroy should not be entertained. We have a responsibility not just for ourselves but our families and strangers, as well. Everyone's life affects someone else.

Amazingly, a diamond stone actually repels mud and dirt. Most foreign substances will not stick to the diamond because of its oily surface. That's right! The oily surface of the diamond allows it to stay free from things that take away its beauty. We can identify diamond-type people by what they allow to cling to them. If we hold a diamond in the dark, it might seem like any other stone. But if we are sensitive to touch, we will feel it has oil. A person filled with the Spirit of God can sense in their spirit the presence of other spirit-filled people because of the presence of the Holy Spirit. People filled with the Spirit of God should not allow the worldly things of life to get into their life. Fleshly attitudes and worldly behavior dry up the anointing the Holy Spirit places in a saint. Oil in the diamond is like the Holy Spirit in the individual. Everyone has to deal with unpleasant stuff. We all have to put up with situations that are less than desirable. We must learn to minister to people in unpleasant situations without allowing the situation or event to take hold of us. Satan is constant in his efforts to get the vices of life attached to us, thereby stealing our walk with the Lord. The Holy Spirit is our oil, and He enables us to repel the dirt of life. We are Christians—ambassadors of the highest God! Life's troubles are not supposed to cling to us. Jesus came that we may have life and life abundant (John 10:10, KJV). We are here to change our environment. The environment is not supposed to change us. Only what we allow can get us down. Christians are to be hard like the diamond yet changeable in the hands of God. We possess a rare and beautiful quality that makes us valuable—the Holy Spirit. With Him we are more than able. We have everything it takes to live in the world without the world living in us. As said before, in the dark a diamond looks like any other stone, but shine a light toward it, and the whole room begins to shine. In the darkest of all situations, we are to sparkle and reflect the light of Jesus. How can we be different? Why should we be different? Because the Living God, the Creator of the universe, is alive in us, His Spirit desperately trying to work through us. "This I say then, Walk in the Spirit, and ye shall not fulfill the lust of the flesh". Galatians 5:16 (KJV) Living with the Holy Spirit guiding us is how a Christian can live differently!

THE PAST IS NOT YOUR FUTURE

*J*acob grew old and realized life was almost over. He gathered his sons to speak with them one last time. Jacob loved these men and saw areas of their lives that needed improvement. His fore sight of the future of their lives inspired him to speak frankly to each son. Jacob had watched each son develop their individual characters since the time of their birth. The future of each son was clear to him, and their behavior needed change. Jacob exercised his responsibility as a father and leader and gave counsel to each son. Jacob had developed wisdom and maturity while walking with the Lord. He became a good judge of character, and he desired the best for each son and their families. Some of his words were hard council, some were warnings to change, and some were blessings for the future. Most everything he said became prophetic in their lives and the tribes they represented.

We can thank God who loves us so much He gave us the Bible. It records Jacob's conversations and others that may be a guide for each of us. As we study the scriptures, the Holy Spirit will lead us to change by convicting us of actions and thoughts that are below standard for the children of God. The Lord reveals habits and characteristics of those that did well and those that did not hit the mark. Every page of scripture and each story recorded is for our learning. Life really does have an instruction manual; it's called the Bible.

Most people can remember a time when someone who counseled them for some reason would say, "If you maintain this course in life, you'll end up..." Each time, those giving counsel could see the future by looking at past and current actions. God brings circumstances and people into our lives that encourage us to see the need for change. Then God always provides us with the resources to make the change. These resources may be elders, Christian counselors, and of course the Bible. Many fathers have not been taught the importance of taking time to exercise the duty of counseling their young, so the responsibility falls to each individual to do a self-examination. We need to take a moment and look back through the events that have occurred in our life and the character we have developed. We will be able to identify much of our character by the way we responded to events in life thus far. Our attitude in times of stress will reveal a lot about our character. The way we behave when challenged with something new is a great indicator. Do we constantly seek praise from others ? Are we in the habit of building others up, or do we belittle others? Do we pray and get insight from God, or is every decision a thought of our own? Do we treat everyone with respect? Do we only favor those who give us honor? Our past decisions—were they good or bad? Why? Did we receive counsel and turn it down, preferring to depend on our own wisdom to lead us ? Are we critical, self-serving, jealous, fearful, or judgmental of others? Is it our nature to forgive others for things we believe to be wrong? Are we known to be compassionate with others? Could others tag us as being apathetic? Are we doing something that would not please God? Whew! That is a lot of negativity now out and in the open. It can be a little depressing, but it must be recognized and dealt with properly. With the information gathered from the past, ask ourselves the question, if I keep the same course, maintain the same pace, and do the same things, will I arrive at a destination that is pleasing to myself and the Lord? We may remember events from years ago that seem as fresh in our memory as if it happened yesterday. Now, with the knowledge of time slipping by so fast, can we afford to put off change any longer? If years gone seem as yesterday, then we should treat our tomorrows with great urgency.

Somewhere between our teenage years and our mid-twenties, most people have developed a pattern in life. One's character has become known to family and friends. Comments like, "I cannot talk to them. They're always so angry," or "They are so easy to get along with," are being said about us by others. It doesn't take long for everyone to know what our day-to-day behavior will include. We are then excluded or included in a circle of people that tolerate our behavior. People who behave or think similarly to ourselves become our friends. Others slip away, never to be heard from again. This of course has an exception of a few family members who must live with us and love us regardless of how we behave.

We have already looked at our character traits. Now take a quick glance at the people we call *friend*. What types of character do we see in our friends? How do they behave in their day-to-day relationships with peers and those in authority? Before we become too critical with all their faults, pause for a moment and think . We may be looking at others who are a mirror image of ourselves. Jesus said in Mark 7:1-5 (KJV) that before we attempt to remove the speck from our friend's eye to check ourselves first, because there may be a log in our own eye. What does this mean? Before we criticize someone else for a fault we think they have, it is important to examine ourselves to see if the same fault exists in our life. We may realize we have the same fault! The Holy Spirit, who is ever so gentle with us, allows us to see a reflection of ourselves in the lives of others. Isn't He merciful! We need to check carefully what we see; it may be God politely presenting our faults to us. What we find distasteful in others, God may find distasteful in us. The fact that He is allowing us to see it speaks of His love and desire for change in us. Looking into the mirror of God's Word and doing a character inspection may be surprising. A question we should ask ourselves is whether we have lowered ourselves to the levels and standards of other people, or are we accepting the challenge to rise up—up to the standard of living that God deems best for us?

The winner of the marathon was not always in the lead from start to finish. At various times and places along the twenty-six mile run, someone else was in front of him. To win, he could not give up doing his best. If he gave up when someone passed him in a spurt of energy, he would have lost the race. Instead he kept pushing hard with the expectancy that he would recover his position in front. He surely did not want to give up the race to discouragement. Discouragement doesn't have a face or legs to run on, and it does not have a trophy room. Discouragement is a dark spirit that will steal the victory from anybody just because it can. Discouragement is much like the playground bully that hits someone just to see them cry. Discouragement takes things from us not because he wants the object but because he delights in seeing us suffer. We must develop the ability to recognize discouragement for what it is and then defeat it with hope and faith.

When discouragement comes, we may feel like someone is kicking us while we are down. That is the devils delight. Being down and being kicked might be true, *but* there is one thing we never want to do when we are in a battle. Never let the enemy think they have a chance of winning. To maintain superiority, we must keep up our courage and always work at keeping the enemy discouraged. My friend, we are on a spiritual battlefield, and our enemy, the devil, will do anything and use anyone to keep us discouraged. He will even use us against ourselves. Therefore it is vital that we guard our thoughts. Our thoughts are secret weapons that when used properly are able to change the course of the fight anytime just by revealing them. We need to stay positive in our thinking; it is the power we need in battle. How? By changing our thoughts into words. Great care should be taken to insure our words are positive and leading to where we want to be, not where we are.

Once a person confided that the car payment was difficult at a particular time due to the lack of income. We prayed for financial help. In church that same day, the pastor gave a really good message on trusting in the Lord. We stretched our faith to believe God would supply the need. Our faith shot off like an arrow into the window of heaven. That same hour I'm sure it was posted in heaven that we trusted God and believed He would send the answer. By initiating prayer we had placed our foot onto the spiritual battlefield. Both the angels of God and the demons of hell could see the course our faith had taken. On the way home, this same person experienced a blown-out tire. The first thought through our minds was this was not the blessing we had hoped for. We don't need more troubles. What we need are solutions. The Spirit of God quickly spoke to my heart. "Do not become discouraged. You have entered the battlefield, and your enemy wants to defeat you in your thoughts and thereby steal your blessing that is on the way. You have shot the weapon of faith. The enemy will shoot the weapon of fear and discouragement." We are to stay positive and maintain hope in the Lord. Within hours, a new tire was purchased and the car payment was made at no cost to this individual.

My friend, additional trouble can be an indication to us that the Lord is at work to answer our prayer. On the battlefield, when we shoot at our enemy, we need to realize that he will shoot back. That is why they call it a battlefield; both parties in the battle are shooting at each other. Prayers with faith that touch the heavens are public information. As with Job, God often displays our faith for all to see. That means both light and darkness can see the aggressive action we have taken. Yes, prayer is an act of aggression against the elements of darkness. Of course the devil is going to retaliate. We have to know in our spirit that God wants good things for us. The act of aggression toward us after we pray is from the enemy. His efforts to discourage us will keep us from our destiny if we allow our eyes to be set on the circumstances. We are to live our lives by faith, not by sight. The real battlefield is in our own thinking. It is imperative that we maintain a positive mind set toward God, His Word, and the promises for a better tomorrow. In Daniel 10:10-17 (KJV), He prayed for twenty-one days; afterward he found out that the reason for the delay in his blessing was that the devil had detained the angel who was carrying his need . Don't give up praying. Our attitude is just as important to receiving the blessing as is the angel that is carrying the blessing. We may have prayed and for much more than twenty-one days with little or no results. We need to check our talk; have we been speaking positively or negatively about the situation? Praying for something to happen and speaking that it will never come to pass is a confused message. As soldiers of faith, our prayers, actions, and words spoken all need to be in unity. That means everything going in the same direction—toward the goal. Try fasting; Daniel was also fasting for those twenty-one days. God will reveal the guidance that is best for us at the time. Fasting is not necessarily done to get the answer's we want. Our focus in fasting should be to hear God's voice on the matter of concern. Until we have heard His voice, we respond by waiting in positive-speaking faith. Our answer is on the way. When He speaks, regardless of what He says, that should become our direction. Sometimes the answer is no; in that case, we should believe He is looking out for our well being and we should accept no as being in our best interest.

In Jacob's last words to Gad, Jacob told him, "A troop shall overcome you, but you shall overcome at the end" (Genesis 49:19, KJV). First we see Gad is to be overcome, that is not good news for anybody to receive. To be told we are going to take a loss of any kind is not what most of us would call encouraging. However, the Bible does say, "A just man will fall seven times" (Proverbs 24:16 KJV). Now the number seven is not a fixed number that we can determine that success begins after the seventh stumble. Rather, it is figurative, indicating we can all expect to fall a perfect number of times. The same verse goes on to say we will rise again. Praise the Lord! It is not the falling that counts; it is the getting back up that separates winners and losers.

In football, the one carrying the ball always endeavors to fall toward his own goal line when he is tackled. Those men are taught that if they're going down, do everything they can do to get closer to the goal on the way down. In life it is certain that we will be knocked down. We only lose if we stay down. If our circumstances indicate we're going down, get close to the Lord, quickly. He will give us insight into the reason we are experiencing trouble. The decision whether to lie down and quit, giving the victory to the invisible uncaring spirit of discouragement, is ours. Or we can get up and fight with the attitude of finishing the course. The faster we get up, the more we intimidate our enemy. The sooner we get up, the closer we are to our destiny. With the Lord on our side, we are stronger than we estimated. We need to develop a "get over it" attitude, dust off our jeans, and charge again. Gad was told he would be overcome, but in the end, *he* would overcome. It was a prophetic promise spoken to him by his father, Jacob. Our prophetic promise to us from our Father in heaven is that "we are more than a conqueror" (Romans 8:37, KJV); "we can do all things through Jesus" (Philippians 4:13, KJV) paraphrased. We may not feel like it right now, but with the Lord, we will overcome all obstacles and accomplish the vision He has placed in us. But it is up to us to get up and take the first steps toward running.

After a set back, we may have more knowledge of what *not* to do versus what to do. Well, with that knowledge at hand, get up and start again. This time, don't do the same thing that caused the downfall. Instead, seek to accomplish life differently. Get alone with the Lord. Turn off the TV, radio, and telephones. Get quiet! Listen to His directions without other worldly sounds interfering. Do things differently, and the results should be different. Try God's plan. It will produce results better than anything we have tried before. With God, we will overcome!

Running the Race

*R*ob remembered the words of his basic training DI: The enemy would take no days off. The enemy would strike when and where the weakest link appeared. Therefore, to be ready for battle, he would have to endure running on both good and bad days. So Rob ran 750 miles, rain or shine, in order to accomplish the run on the day of the race. The team captain reminded the team many times that if they were serious about this endeavor, they had to maintain the personal desire to accomplish the run. No one would hold their hand.

One day during training, a technique was taught that would help a weary runner resume running after an unscheduled stop. It could happen that after expending the energy needed to run the first twenty miles, the body may not have sufficient strength to start running again. This is due to the physical drain that the body experiences when pushed beyond normal limits. Muscles do not respond as quickly to the same commands as they do when the body is fresh. But there are methods to overcome a fatigued state if one really wanted to run again. One method taught was to thrust the arm up and outward, kind of like throwing a punch at the sun. "Punching the sun," alternating first one hand and then the other, would cause a pull in the leg muscles, which in turn would work toward restoring muscle memory. The team laughed and had a great time during the class when this was taught. No one really believed they would have to use such methods. After all, they were soldiers and were accustomed to running. Plus, they were young and thought themselves invincible.

After months of training, the day finally arrived to run the real race. The night prior to the race, everyone went to the registration building to obtain their runner numbers and weigh in. Weigh in is always a humbling experience. Somehow the scales make us think we should have done more. As Rob stepped up on the scales, the young lady operating the scale looked at his weight of 196 pounds, of which he was very proud, and said to the recorder, "Clydesdale." Immediately Rob took note of the label of being called a work horse. In a fun sort of way, he commented to the young lady that it was not good to discourage the runners before the race.

Rob did not see himself as a work horse. He saw himself ranking up there with the World Cup running horses—whatever type they were. Rob admitted he did not think he would win, but he did think of himself a bit faster than a workhorse. He had lost twenty to twenty-five pounds getting ready for this event. He felt he had invested much or suffered much to lose weight in the training so that he could run the distance. She smiled and assured him it was only a title given to the heavier runners, meaning nothing more than the class and position of runners he would be joining at the start. The Clydesdale types were to start the race in the back, behind the slimmer, faster runners.

After weigh in, the team went out to eat. Arriving at a pizza restaurant, the leader announced he was paying, and he was also ordering. He expected everyone to enjoy his selection. *Everyone loves pizza. How bad can it be if he orders?* ran through Rob's mind until the dinner arrived. Spaghetti was served without any topping at all. To Rob's surprise, it was bad—worse than he had expected. Of all the foods Rob disliked most, pasta was at the top of the list. Here it was, served without any kind of topping, no meatballs, and no sauce. Nothing! Now he sat looking at this huge plate heaped up with nothing but pasta. *Yuck, yuck, yuck.* The team leader reminded everyone about putting the proper foods into the body. This was the night to load the body up with fresh carbohydrates. Pushing fresh carbohydrates into the body just before the run would provide a great reserve of energy for the body. In the morning, the stress of the race would consume all normal supplies. Rob ate the whole plate, thinking, *Doesn't pizza bread contain carbohydrates? Bread is a carb, is it not?* The colonel was quick in his response to what everyone was thinking. There are different types of carbohydrates; some are better than others. For the team to do well, he wanted the best.

The team was up early and ready to run the morning of the race. Certain things can bother a person on long race days that are not often talked about. What if you have to go to the bathroom along the way? Where does one go, especially on a run like this through the city of Washington, DC? This may sound humorous to those not faced with the situation, but to a runner focused on doing well and finishing a race, this is an important factor to consider. Will there be time, and will a place be available when faced with this important event? Rob decided to take care of this business before starting the run.

Starting the run was exhilarating. Rob could feel the emotion of the crowd. Thirteen thousand runners all lined up to run. Rob was very excited and found a place in the middle. The front was reserved for the slimmer, faster runners. The race officials must have thought the heavier, Clydesdale types would be a hindrance to the lightweights; therefore, they wanted them in the rear. But Rob thought it best to start closer to the finish. After all, he needed all the help he could get. The gun sounded, and everyone began to run! Miles were passing very quickly. By the time Rob crossed the seventh mile marker, he realized he was running too fast for his physical condition. He had trained to run ten-minute miles. That is not very fast in the world of running, but Rob's vision was to finish. To Rob, this was a race of endurance. At this point he was actually running seven-minute miles, which was much too fast for him. Rob realized he had to slow down or risk not finishing the run. He had not trained to move that fast. At mile thirteen, he had finally slowed down to the speed he had trained at to endure the entire twenty-six miles. It felt good to settle into his own running pace, and he began to enjoy himself.

Running in the capital city of our nation was exciting! He had not seen much of the city before, so it was new and interesting to see the sites along the way. His mind was occupied with all the buildings and people he passed. Rob also felt encouraged by the people who cheered the runners on and by the dedication of the hosting staff. Some passed out water or rehydrating-type drinks, and others offered salve for aching muscles.

Everyone alive has started the race of life. The trouble is that many are running toward the wrong goal. It could be at this point we realize that the direction we are taking will not lead us to the desired destination. The good news is that it's not too late to change directions. Great thing about running with the Lord is that it's not important when or where you start; it's all about where you finish. The book of Revelation instructs us to be zealous and repent (Revelation 3:19, KJV) (that means be eager to turn around and go the right direction), and to those who overcome these obstacles, He will allow to sit with Him on His throne (Revelation 3:21, KJV). It's satisfying to know God allows U turns and builds on-ramps anytime someone wants to run with Him.

Apostle Paul wrote that everyone who enters the race to run should run with purpose, set his mind to endure, count the cost, determine to finish, and reach for the prize (1 Corinthians 9:24, KJV). With this in mind, have you developed a goal in life that includes God? Jesus is the only one that can take us to the finish. In the race of life, no one crosses the winners' line without God.

So many things never get finished. Circumstances change, and we must leave some things undone. So it is with us, but not with God. Our relationship with God is *not* one of the things we can afford to leave undone. God will do His part to insure we are supplied with all we need to run with Him. Without Him we will experience difficulties and old-fashioned discouragement that may deter our successes. But with God, we will be in the winners' circle at the end.

Our enemy the devil has come to kill, steal, and destroy (John 10:10, KJV). He will take no days off, no holidays, no rest days, not even an hour will we go unwatched by the demons of darkness. If the evil one can discourage us and bring us to the point of not trying again, he has won the battle. I don't say this to scare anyone but rather to encourage everyone to enter the race and stay in the race, lest their time to run expire. I challenge everyone to never, ever give up the right to run the race of life towards eternal life. By not choosing Jesus, we forfeit the chance of winning a position in the kingdom of God. Simply by doing nothing, our position will be lost. Start right now. It is never too late.

In our Christian walk, it too is easy to fall into a rut of not seeking to improve ourselves. Once we acknowledge Jesus is Lord, we may have the tendency to think we have completed the mission. Praying and receiving Jesus is only the beginning. There is so much more to learn and do. During stressful times it may become difficult to keep attending worship. In most cases, no one will call and instruct us to attend for our own good and future growth. These are times we must walk in discipline; it's our life and our responsibility to stay in the race. To run and finish well, we must maintain our time with the Lord . It will be important to eat well in times of difficulty more so than at other times. Consume the Word of God, it provides the strength needed to endure the difficult seasons life puts in our way.

Books inform us a great deal of what God wants for us. Books can help explain difficult passages of scripture. But there is no substitute for the Holy Bible, God's Word. It is alive and powerful and is able to be relied on to give us life. Only the Bible can be there in time of need. It is a faithful source of energy, insight, and healing. God will not share this ability with any other book, no matter how appealing the author or the subject might be. At times we may prefer something else, but the real thing is always best.

Scripture encourages us to make amends with our adversaries quickly (Matthew 5:25, KJV), and in another verse, it says that today is the day of salvation (2 Corinthians 6:2, KJV). If there are things in our lives that do not measure up to what God desires for us, we need to get rid of that stuff now. Life takes so many unexpected turns, and time is so unforgiving. It is always best to do what we can today. Time and resources beyond this moment are not guaranteed, and the same opportunities may never arrive again. Once we start the day, there may not be a place or time afforded to take care of such important business—important business being salvation of our souls, forgiveness for sins committed against God and others, and telling another of the saving grace of Jesus.

Sometimes the excitement of others cheering us on in life can cause us to get ahead of what we are equipped to do. Trying to keep up with others may not be possible. Attempting to do some great thing before we are properly trained could cause heartache. Training can take time, and seeking God's direction can sometimes be frustrating. We tend to lack patience and skip the training. We all will do better when we wait on the Lord and get the training. Don't get discouraged. Once God opens up the path we are to run, it will happen quickly. It will be difficult at times to remember our purpose and remain focused on the main thing. Recalling what we originally set out to accomplish is important; that is why God said to write it down. To be the fastest or largest does not mean we will be the most effective. Some important questions we must ask ourselves include: are we personally going to be enriched through this adventure in our life? Will we have a positive impact in the lives of our family and others God has placed us with? It will not matter how fast or how much we do anything if at the end of life, we are not found to be in fellowship with God. The life spent out of fellowship with God will be a failure.

Well-meaning saints sometimes encourage others to get involved in doing some task they believe is good. Too often the people encouraged to do these tasks do not do as well as expected. Consequently these people feel as though they failed. The first step anyone should take in any adventure is to take it to the Lord. Before jumping into anything, it is important to ask if this is what God has instructed us to do. We are anointed to do a particular thing for His glory. In that particular thing, we will not fail!

Don't—*don't*—miss what God has ordained you to do. God ordains us to do certain things so that we will be effective for Him and finish the race of life victoriously.

Oh No!

Twenty-one miles behind him, things were going great. Rob was having a good running day. Then he saw a fellow team member struggling. He was staggering back and forth as if he had been drinking. He had hit that invisible wall that runners talk about. He had pushed himself beyond his limits for too long. His ability to maneuver was seriously impaired. He was no longer effective in running this race. He would require a time of rest and rejuvenation before he could run again.

Rob felt compelled to assist him to the aid station, which was only a few yards away, but in doing so, he had to stop running. Guiding his friend into the aid station took just a few moments. His friend safely deposited in the hands of professional help, Rob turned to continue the run. But his legs did not want to move as they had before. There he was, less than five miles to the finish line, and he could not get started. Rob realized that something was wrong. He did not have the "get up and go" that he had started with. His energy was spent. His legs would not respond to the commands his mind was giving. Rob began to experience a sinking feeling. Rob began to think he had just messed up. Helping his teammate was stealing his dream of finishing the marathon. If he had not been ill, if he had not been stumbling, Rob would not have stopped to assist him. Rob would have been at least a mile closer to the finish line by now.

Rob began to search for who was at fault. His first thought was to wonder why the first aid team didn't come out to the road and help him. Then, why didn't his teammate stop and rest before he became incoherent? At that moment his hopes were falling. He was searching to blame others for not succeeding. Rob's legs would not respond, and the best he could do now was walk, and it was a slow walk with his heart continuing to sink. A voice in his head was saying, "That act of kindness has cost you your dream. Seven hundred and fifty miles of training…for what? For nothing!" All the training was wasted just because he had compassion on someone else. Rob was not satisfied with this outcome. Plus he was embarrassed by the way he was thinking about his teammate. The bottom line was that Rob felt like he had failed. Why would God bring him this far and not enable him to finish? That made no sense. He thought back to the days he was tired and walked home or the times he had even hitched a ride. He should have trained harder. His thoughts dwelt on the starting line of how he was not in the proper place that he was assigned as a Clydesdale runner. Could this failure be his fault for being disobedient? Maybe he could have worked wiser and harder. A million thoughts were racing into his mind of what he should have or could have done. The finish line was only about five miles away. It was difficult to accept that he was not going to finish the race running.

In difficult times, we have a tendency to blame ourselves or others for setbacks in life. We should be aware that sometimes what we think is failure is not failure at all. These times of difficulty may only be temporary stops or pauses to improve us for tomorrow. Setbacks may be a set up by the Lord to improve our position at the finish. A mistaken thought we often have is that the race of life compares with the races we see run around tracks at the local sports arena. The race in life is not about the fastest or even having the most. The race of life is all about quality and the development of a relationship with God. It also includes those we may influence to abide in Him. Improving our relationship while we are here in this earthly vessel is a lifelong adventure. As we get older, we begin or have begun to see the importance of being in tune with God. That might be because we think we are closer to meeting Him at age fifty than we are at age twenty. Could be the years of trials and tribulations cause one to think on what is really important in life? For many it is the promise recorded in God's Word: children trained up under His Word will not depart from it (Proverbs 22:6, KJV). Time and again we hear this promise fulfilled, praise the Lord! Thus credit needs to be given to God, godly parents, or grandparents for teaching and praying family members into the kingdom of God. Did they pray because they had nothing else in life to do? No, they prayed because over the years they found out what really works! The truly important things in life are found in a relationship with Jesus. People who want a better life for their loved ones run to the Lord with their treasures. The collection of plastic toys and wooden houses will not satisfy the needs of the soul now or ever. A relationship with God is worth more than anything this world has to offer. The wise person will always choose God when choices are to be made, even if the choice means facing a difficulty. God will reward the faithful.

Sometimes our "Oh no!" instances in life are turned into, "Oh, my! Look what the Lord has done for me!" There are hundreds of testimonies, thousands of lives being radically changed for the better after an "oh no." At times we become comfortable in the way things are. It becomes hard to see that what God has in store for us is so much better. God allows us to make decisions that will place us in positions of discomfort. These moments are meant to stir our hearts. When we find our situation uncomfortable, we are more apt to look to the Lord questioning and seek change. In the search, we find God has prepared greater things if we are willing to change and live life His way. Good changes are waiting for those who will look up and trust in the Lord!

There are times we get to moving a little too fast for our own welfare. Troubles along the way tend to slow us down, but they don't have to become stop signs. Instead, trouble may be a speed bump set in place to slow us down and cause us to look around to see something important. America doesn't have many speed bumps on the roads we travel, but in some countries, speed bumps are an effective tool used to protect the public from fast-moving traffic. Speed bumps also provide the traveler a great place to take a break, check the load, and review their progress. In some countries speed bumps offer a place for vendors to display their treasures. During the pause, you can decide to buy their products or move on. Slowing down once in a while allows us time to consider where we are and what the road looks like before us.

Do we really have life all under control, or could this latest bump in life's road be an opportunity to change our direction? To adjust our load? What are we carrying in our hearts as truth? Are the principles we are living by the very best for the family? Does God have us in this position to help or be helped? Nothing happens by accident. Has God set up this moment so we can stop and take inventory? What are we to do for the Lord right now? How can He work through us at this very moment?

Our memories can often provide a clearer picture of how God works in our life. Looking at these memories, we can also see how He set us up for the last blessing. So it is right now, God is busy setting us up for the next big blessing. Every event somehow leads to Him receiving the glory through our lives. Every moment of every day is a set up to do something that will determine a better tomorrow. The question we must ask ourselves is how will we respond to the situation we are in right now. Remember, the situation may not be about us; it could be all about God working through us. This may be a time that God has planned as a test to see if we have grasped the lessons He has taught through his great servants. This could be the moment to put into practice what we have been learning. The teacher is most often silent during the test. Be strong. Be of good courage. Pray about the next good choice we will make. God is getting us ready to move forward.

LION'S VOICE

*A*s Rob walked along the marathon course, he began to consider all that had transpired. Questions entered his mind like, *Am I going to let the devil convince me it is all over and quit?* That thought was not very appealing. Rob wanted to believe God could give him strength even now at this point when he had spent more energy than ever before. After all, God is the God of impossibilities. It was God who helped him train. God was there each day with words of encouragement. It was God who confirmed the vision in his heart, was it not? Rob could still see himself running across the finish line. Rob began to believe he could run again regardless of the circumstances. Rob started to speak to his problem. He had a great God who could overcome anything. Rob's God could give him more energy and strength. The God Rob had was not dependent on anything worldly. He was God, and He alone could enable Rob to run.

Continuing to follow the life of Gad and the Gadites, we read Deuteronomy 33:20-21. Jacob and his son Gad have been dead for about 400 years, and now Moses is also ready to die. Jacob's sons have grown into tribes. The Gadite tribe at this time consisted of thousands of men and women. The thirteen tribes collectively are called the nation of Israel. Moses has taken Israel as close to the land of promise as God would allow. Just a few days before Israel crosses the Jordan River, Moses takes one last opportunity to speak to the tribes that he has led, trained, and encouraged to conquer this new territory.

Moses began by describing Gad as one who dwells as a lion (Deuteronomy 33:20-21, KJV). To dwell as a lion is to describe a king—one who conquers and rules in his particular domain. The apostle Paul challenges us a different way. He says that we are more than conquerors through Christ (Romans 8:37, KJV). Peter calls us a royal priesthood (1 Peter 2:9, KJV). All three, conquerers, royalty, and priest, are describing the chosen children of God. The inspired words recorded by each of these men should motivate us to live by a higher standard. Royalty does not live by the standards set by those living around them. Royalty chooses a high standard of living, and people around them attempt to live the same way. God has a standard of living that is holy and high. He has invited us to live this standard through Jesus. Sadly many Christians today have only used Jesus as a fire escape plan, calling on His name for salvation from hell's fiery flames, but neglecting to live life by the standard He and His Father have given us in Scripture. The worldly person will think in terms of having material things to make them a success. God thinks in terms of holy living as successful living. Does our strength and sense of success come from stuff or from living in harmony with biblical principles written by the Lord?

A lion cub is playful and carefree. Being a youth, they depend greatly on the parent for protection and provision. The fully grown lion has been taught to hunt and live effectively. Grown lions have gained knowledge of their strength and power. Each paw is moved with authority and confidence. A grown lion knows how to fight.

Gadite men were highly trained individuals, experts in war with the shield and sword, and as swift as gazelles (1 Chronicles 12:8, RSV). As Christians we are to become confident with our faith and experts in Scripture. Both the lion and the gazelle are given as examples to help us build our lives. We now have the gazelle added to help us see the additional abilities of the Gadite men. Gazelles indeed run very fast, but speed is not their greatest quality. What brings our attention to the gazelles is the amazing ability to dart sideways while running to avoid a hazard. As we run through life, traps of temptation are laid out to snare us. God's Word will give us the ability to recognize and avoid temptation. Learning the art of stepping aside to let sinful traps lie will only come from time with the Lord.

We must learn to wield our sword, quickly and with the precision of an expert. God's Word, the scripture written in the Bible, is our sword. Too often we leave our sword in its scabbard and experience loss from the attacks of evil by never putting up a fight. God gave us the Scripture to live by and use in life's battles. Our victories will be determined by what we do with the Word of God. God has given each of us a sword. This sword is more powerful than any manmade weapon. Scripture is to be spoken toward your troubles, believing in God's Word over our own understanding. Trusting God's Word is the foundation of victorious living. We should feel free to pull our sword out of its scabbard and wield it against anything that hinders our walk in life. People of faith are quick to speak the promises of God in any situation and quick to share what God can do. Boasting of the great exploits we have done is pride-filled living. Speaking of what God can do is faith-filled living. God's Word becomes both a sword and a shield when spoken. What God can do becomes a shield against fear and doubt when spoken. The key here is that we have to speak. Speaking God's Word is like erecting an invisible shield that we stand behind. The world may not see it, but that does not mean it is not there.

Confidant living as a godly king requires meekness. Moses was a meek man. In fact, the Bible records that he was the meekest man to ever live (Numbers 12:3, KJV). The nation Israel, which was estimated to be 2,000,000 people strong, was led through the wilderness by the meekest man ever to live. That is not something a mousey man could do. Meekness is not being mousey. A good way to interpret meekness is having power under control. Moses had power and his power was under control. Jesus, the Lion of the Tribe of Judah, lived a meek life. He could have called upon angels to His defense, but he came to do a work for His Father. Because of His desire to please His Father and His compassion for us, He kept His power under control. When we decide to honor the Lord with all our thoughts and actions, we can have real power. Part of having power under control is controlling our emotions when faced with adversities. Peter described Christians as being kings and priests. These are positions of power and influence. Christians who take up this challenge are to be harnessed by the Spirit of God. Behaving like the devil all week and acting very saintly on Sunday should not be considered as having power under control. Sunday best behavior only would really be called acting, and we have enough actors. True Christians live by a higher, different standard, trusting in God's Word every day and not giving in to the desires of the flesh.

According to Moses, Gad would tear the arm with the crown of the head. The arm represents an army, and the crown represents the leader of that army. Holy Spirit-filled believers are to have dominion over the army of darkness, *demons,* and the head of that army, which is Satan. This authority is given to us by Jesus, who conquered all darkness through His shed blood on the cross. We are to war against the works of darkness. God has given each of us talents and gifts that enable us to minister life and light to others. We are to use these talents to free sinners caught in sin's trap. Our fight is to be spiritual, not physical. How do we accomplish this without attacking people? By using our voice, we can speak positive life into those that are bound. In other words, we are to use our voice and say out loud what it is we want the misbehaving person to do. Repeating what a person is doing wrong only serves to support the wrong behavior. Words do have power according to the Bible (Proverbs 18:21, KJV). Positive words build, and positive godly actions are needed for better living in the future. What prevents us from doing this privileged task? Fear and ignorance!

Fear—of losing material things or fear of being called a zealot, for example—is one factor that prevents us from stepping into this ministry, a very valuable ministry God has offered to all of us. Fear of not succeeding also prevents many from ever trying. Fear sounds like, *What if I really did not hear God's voice? I'll look like a fool.* Fear of what others may think incarcerates those who submit to it. A lion living in the jungle is fearless. He knows he is a ruler in his particular domain. You don't see them sparring with the other lions. Lions choose not to strut or boast of their abilities. A lion is seldom moved by the speech of other creatures. In fact, just the opposite is true; all of creation close to him is moved by his speech. When at the zoo, it is always thrilling to witness the power displayed when the lions speak. When the lions roar, the block buildings vibrate. That, my friend, is power! That same power is in each Holy Spirit-filled Christian when we speak. Maybe the room does not vibrate physically as with the lion, but rest assured, the spirit world does. Spiritually, not only does it vibrate, it initiates a change that affects everything physically. Darkness takes note of real spirit-led speech and is forced to react. When Spirit-led Christians speak, angels of heaven rise up and await commands from our Lord, seeking directions of how they may assist the one who has spoken in faith. A lion-type person is confident of his position with God. He is sure that everything in his life has come from God, and what he will obtain will be by God's divine hand. No one can take his stuff, and another cannot move into his place unless God allows it. Mature lions live in confidence.

We the believers have been given the opportunity to possess real power and be under control. We are not to spend our energies fighting over stuff and worthless status. God created us to be so much more! We have all been offended or lost our tempers over material things only to find out it was God's plan to move us onto something better. Usually after the fact and after the difficulty, we can look back with embarrassment, and we can see He was in charge of every detail. Well, God is still in charge today. He has not lost sight of us or our needs now or in the future. He desires good stuff in our life but not at the expense of our souls. God is working to bring His plan for us to reality. We are the only ones who could possibly stand in the way.

The greatest fight in life will be with oneself. It is not the enemy we must conquer first but the inner *me* that must first see the victory. Without a vision, people parish (Proverbs 29:18, KJV). What do you see? Who are you? God has chosen you and has a plan for you! (Jeremiah 29:11, KJV) If we see ourselves defeated, we most likely will be. If we see ourselves having victory over anything, there is always the possibility we will. We were created in His image to be a kingly, conquering, taking-the-promised-land kind of people. Satan himself cannot stand in our way. Think for a moment of the power our God has made available to us. To say to the mountain, "Move," and it shall move. (Matthew 21:21, KJV). One reason we do not speak to our situations is we are self-conscious of who is watching us. What will others think if they see us talking to... our problems? It is acceptable to speak about our problems, but we have a great deal of trouble speaking to objects that hinder us. So we find ourselves in the position of attempting to deal with our problems in a fashion that does not embarrass us with our group of peers. Often our greatest, most critical, and most effective condemner is ourselves. Wouldn't it be better to be identified with our Lord and enjoy victory over life's troubles? It's time to stop rehearsing our problems and begin proclaiming God's promise to conquer all! Put troubles on notice that soon our God will be overcoming each and every issue.

Speaking to trouble can be a difficult thing to do. For example, I lived in the wilderness regions of Mexico a few years ago without the benefit of a telephone. Calling anyone meant an hour drive to the nearest town. One day we were offered a rural cellular phone that would connect our Bible school with the rest of the world. To say we were excited is an understatement. We paid an enormous price for the phone but felt it was worth the cost. It turned out to be very problematic. Every problem meant a trip to town to resolve the issue. One spring while conducting Bible school, the phone was very important to us. We had developed the mindset that this plastic instrument should serve us well. It was not holding up to its end of the deal. One particular week it took traveling to town every day just to maintain telephone commutations. As the week progressed, I began to be angry over the phone problems. I also began to share with others my negative thoughts about the telephone. On the fourth or fifth day of the week, I arrived at the telephone company office after a long ride and much prayer, trying to calm the anger I believed to be caused by this instrument. Praying all the way to town, I was asking God to reveal why we had all this trouble. I wanted to be free and turn all my attention toward ministering in the school. I walked into the office, and a man who, to the best of my knowledge, was not a believer looked at me and said, "My friend, it is almost as if a demon has possessed your phone. You need to get rid of it." He was speaking of course about the demon. It was the voice of God using this man. I knew instantly God was speaking to me. Oh yes, the individual was speaking, but there are times you just know that God is using their mouth to give a message to you. This was one of those times. I returned home thinking, *How can I speak to a piece of plastic? What difference could it possibly make?* I waited until no one was around. I was very self-conscious and stepped up to the phone. I rebuked the darkness that was influencing it. Then I went on to describe the method of great work it would perform from that day forth. Glory to God! From that day on and for years after, it was never a problem. In fact, that piece of plastic became an instrument of blessing many times over.

What issue, problem, or trouble is in our life that needs to be told about the greatness of our God? A lion will roar to establish and secure his territory. It is time to speak and establish our territory. His Word causes everything to change, and He has given us the privilege and power to use it as we speak.

First at the Table

*A*s Rob walked and prayed along the course of the marathon, he noticed many runners at this point in the race sitting on the side lines. They were now involved with taking refreshments and chit-chat. The run had become difficult. Many lacked the motivation to continue. No doubt they were led by someone or something to enter this event. Now after twenty plus miles and some difficulties, the run was not as important as it had been in the beginning. The direction held at the start was now replaced by something easier and less strenuous. The reason to continue was shaded by temporal items of personal comfort. Sadly, no one was there to provide encouragement to the individual runner.

The beginning words of Deuteronomy 33:21 indicate that Gad provided the best or first part for himself.

CHARLES R. ROBINSON

This sounds very selfish to the untrained ear. I pray
God reveals to all of us the value in feeding ourselves
first. Our first reaction is that we should feed others
first. We may see a need in the life of others and feel
it's our duty to provide what they lack even if it costs
us. This may be true in the realm of physical food. But
when it comes to spiritual food, this is a dark, deceptive
lie. In our families and ministries, we often look out
for the flock before ourselves. Parents deeming that the
young ones need Jesus send their children to church yet
stay home themselves. Church leaders send others to
conferences, believing they are too valuable to the day-
to-day operation of the church to leave it unattended
for a few days. In Exodus 34:28 (KJV), we see Moses
left an estimated two million people in the wilderness
while he went up on a mountain. He felt he needed
to converse with God. God, who knows everything
about all people, chose to keep him there for forty days.
Evidently God thinks it is important for us to spend
time with Him. In 1 Samuel 30 (KJV), David returned
to Ziklag to find the women and children had been
taken captive. The men in his charge were so devastated
by the loss that they could not function. In the mist
of all this, David took time to search for the Lord's
leading. If these men with all their responsibilities took
time out for the Lord, so should we.

Leaders of all levels have been guilty of giving time,
resources, and energy to the tending of others before
themselves. This sounds noble and often is praised by
the church and fellow ministers. My friend, it is wrong,
and it is sinful. As leaders, parents, and ministers of

God, we must first spend time in the presence of God every day—*every day*—to receive direction for ourselves as well as others. Our priorities should be God first and family and ministry second. How can we lead if we are not first led? Led by God! A hard question we all need to ask ourselves is just who is leading our day-to-day decisions. The direction I am leading my family or ministry, is it from God or from the circumstances of today? Some might say, "If you knew the work I have to do, you would understand why I have no time for myself or idle hours for waiting on God."

When a friend first stepped into the ministry years ago, he had a vision of spending every morning with the Lord, thinking that after hours of prayer and study, he would then tend to the ministry of the day. One can almost hear people saying, "A pastor only works three hours a week. How can they not have time with God?" However, this ministry started off at six thirty a.m. and ran until late in the evening. After a season of ministry, he and some other ministers gathered together to reflect on the work accomplished and take a day of rest. The summer was spent winning souls, building churches, and leading others toward the Lord. Everyone was excited that hundreds had prayed to receive Jesus as their Lord. By the numbers, it was a great year. The kingdom of God had grown. Everyone was pleased with the outcome and was making plans for another great year to follow. A fellow minister came to bring a word of encouragement. In his message God led him to speak of being busy versus drawing close to the Lord in order to be busy about the correct things.

The Holy Spirit convicted this friend of how far he had strayed away from the Lord. He was heart broken; his spiritual well was dry. Oh, he had been praying, but as time went on, his prayers were shorter and less dependent on the Lord. He studied, but mostly to obtain a message to preach. He worked hard at being a blessing, ensuring every item of need was on hand each day. He was filled with the pride of organizing great events that went off without a single shortfall. The people he worked with were impressed many times because he thought of everything. Messages were built with head knowledge of Scripture or copied from other ministers. It was easy to change voice level and include a few actions, and most everyone called it "the anointing." That was so far from the truth. He had removed himself from meeting with the Lord daily.

But here at the end of the ministry year, he had not grown closer to God. In fact, he felt he was farther away! The fellowship with the Lord was almost gone. Sure, he was doing and saying the right things. No one could tell he was not in the correct place spiritually with the Lord. He repented of letting ministry take first position and vowed to change his priorities.

Much is said about the anointing these days. Various ministers are said to be anointed one day and then a short while later found in the newspaper having been caught living in some sinful life style, their downfall driving souls away from the kingdom by their sinful actions. These men and women were not in daily fellowship with the Lord. Are they saved? Possibly.

Did they preach the truth? Yes, but the messages were stirred up from within themselves. It is not hard to say good things bout the Lord; the question is, are we saying what God wants said? My friend, we cannot live with sinful practices and be in fellowship with God at the same time. The unction of the Holy Spirit only comes from time in God's presence. If we are not walking with the Lord daily, we will have trouble recognizing His voice. We may have much to say, but is it from the Lord?

What's the difference between the anointing and unction, you ask? The difference is that with the anointing, we sense the presence of the Lord. But when unction is present, we are *confronted* by His presence. The anointing we can ignore, but unction forces a decision. There is no place to turn. It is a face-to-face encounter with the Holy Spirit of God. Unction stops us right where we are and confronts us with some aspect of our life, and we must make a decision. To follow Him at that moment or turn away from His guidance.

People who speak with unction only do so by spending time in the Lord's presence. As we dig toward the origin of the word *unction*, we will find that part of the word's makeup in theological word studies of the Old and New Testaments, it includes "something borrowed." Unction is something borrowed that can never be owned because there is only one, and it belongs to the Lord. It cannot be fabricated, developed, or remanufactured by anyone. God is the sole owner of unction. Unction is something God loans to those who spend time with Him. When used, it is always for someone else, and it is never for one's personal use. Unction *always* changes lives.

All around us, marriages are failing, people are so discouraged they commit suicide, and thousands of young and old are bound for the flames of hell by their lifestyles. If we find value in anything, we must spend time with God. To successfully lead others, we must first be led. Putting others first has produced people full of selfish expectancy waiting to be served. That may sound great if we're the one being served, but what can a person really give if they have not been in the presence of God? A morsel of food that is soon consumed or an item of comfort that rots away. Our families and our ministries deserve more. They need instruction that produces and encourages life. This instruction only comes from God.

Many saints are leaving the churches they once attended. We all should be distressed by this and ask why. Why are those who were once faithful to attend church now no longer assembling together. Most reasons boil down to, "We felt like we were not being fed anymore." Now, that may be partly an individual problem and the leadership, but the root on both sides can be followed back to no individual time with the Lord. Whether it be teacher or student or both, neglecting God's presence will produce the same result. The lost people (those not saved) need to be told the saving message of Jesus. Without the presence of the Holy Spirit in their lives, they cannot digest anything life producing. The church body, once it is saved, needs to be taught more than a salvation message to contend with life. Salvation is just the beginning. Then we all need to be taught how to fight the fight of life. Youth need more than "I said so," or "It's in your Bible." We have leaders and parents who repeat, "Someone said one time," or say statements like, "Somewhere in the Bible." What is needed is a word that comes from the Lord. Those phrases "somewhere in the Bible" may be good at one time or another, but our norm should be, "Today the Lord revealed to me." We cannot blame others for our not having spent time near His voice today. It is our choice.

The fight to maintain time with God is a tough battle. Elements of darkness will use everything and anyone to deter this relationship. It is our responsibility to plan our day carefully. What period of time is best to be alone and not hurried with God? The wise will establish a time for prayer and study that will develop into a routine. It is best to choose a time when the fewest distractions are possible. It is important to remember that this time established is set aside to hear the voice of the Lord. He will best be heard in a quiet and still period. The radio, television, or others can be distracting, causing you to miss His word for you. Cell phones, iPads, or any other entertainment devices may be distracting, as well. Turn these things off. Why hinder our opportunity to hear the voice of the Most High God? By silencing these devises, we show honor toward the most holy and powerful God. He is to be revered above all other creatures and causes.

Having a family devotion time with a full schedule can be frustrating. In our zeal to do the right thing, we end up being preachers of the Word and not living examples of the Word. No one wants to be preached at. However, most people do have a desire to hear what the Bible says. Most interesting to all ages is how we live the scriptures we read. So what do we do to make the time pleasant and productive? How can we present the truths of Scripture and have these truths followed by others? One answer is to share what God has placed in our heart, not in the book we hold. Let me say that again differently: Share what God has told us in our private devotions each day. Everyone wants to hear how our Bible has placed freedoms, promises, and victories in our life. Couple that with living what the Bible says, and many more of our family members will grasp it for themselves. The question remains, will we lead them after first being led?

Using biblical information to control people usually does not produce the best results. People rebel when they feel manipulated. Our work should be the works of the Spirit, ministering to set people free, not placing them under condemnation or giving them a list of man made rules to follow. Gad took the first part for himself; he spent time with God and God exalted him to positions of authority. Once in authority, Gad used his position to build, not divide. He did not exalt himself to be king. He did all he could to support the King. Your time with the Lord each day will have great rewards if your purpose is to build God's kingdom.

How we use what God has taught us is very important. The time invested with the Lord and shared with others will be revealed in the life of the listeners. Jesus spent time with the Father and stated that He spoke nothing but what the Father spoke into Him (John 12:49, KJV). I'm sure He had thoughts of His own, but He chose instead to speak the Lord's words above His own. He changed the lives of the disciples and countless others by His obedience in spending time alone with the Father. He came to set the captives free. John 8:36 (KJV) says, "If the Son therefore shall make you free, ye shall be free indeed."

We have all been in situations where those leading a study read word by word from a lesson book that has been prepared by someone else. Sometimes these individuals have great reading abilities while others often stumble as they read the sentences. This method of teaching is often very boring, and the listener's mind wanders to other thoughts. It also speaks a message that the one teaching did not care to prepare. What reason would an individual have for not preparing beforehand? Do they really believe what they're saying, or does the subject and position not hold importance in their life? It is a great privilege and responsibility to teach others about the works of our Lord. We should want our listeners to be so interested that they ask for more. Get alone with God and His Word; study something that has meaning to you and the student. Then share that information from your heart. If you have different points to bring out and need help remembering the order, by all means make an outline.

Let those God has placed in your path hear your heart. Speaking what God spoke to you will cause you to be a more effective minister.

RUNNING WHERE? WITH WHOM?

*A*s Rob walked, he heard runners speaking of the difficulties of the run. The distance of twenty-six miles was easier to talk about than to run out. Many who spoke negatively dropped out of the run. Rob had observed this behavior during the early training days as well. When the colonel first invited everyone to run, there were twenty or more who took the challenge. By race day that number was less than half. Rob knew he had to get started again and hook up with runners that were positive and going in the direction he wanted to go. To entertain negative thoughts or to take a break at this point would be a dangerous thing to do, the danger being that he might convince himself to quit by his own thoughts and speech. He knew that when he was stressed or weary, it wouldn't take too much convincing to drop out of the race. Even though Rob was walking, he chose to identify with the runners instead of those who submitted to weariness and personal comforts. He was praying for strength and speaking words of encouragement to himself. Sure, he was wondering why all this transpired, but he was also sure God had a plan. Rob kept remembering Romans 8:28 (KJV): "And we know that all things work together for good to them that love God, to them who are the called according to his purpose." He had to believe something good was about to happen.

While living in the wilderness, Gad, Rueben, and Simeon were united under the same flag, *living and working close by each other.* As they approached the promised land, these tribes decided to change. Gad and Rueben decided to drop Simeon and unite together with half the tribe of Manasseh.

Without going into great detail, the character of Rueben was unstable as water, being up one day and down the next. He had trouble maintaining direction. Simeon was cruel, mean, and spiteful. He was a danger to be around when he lost his temper, and it appears he was unwilling to change. Gad without a doubt learned great lessons while wandering with these tribes for forty years. At the point of crossing into the promised land, Gad decided to continue his relationship with Rueben but exchanged Simeon for one half the tribe of Manasseh. The name Manasseh means "forgetful." Joseph, his father, in choosing this name, placed a constant reminder in his family to forget the past and live for the future. Gad and Rueben quite possibly continued to learn from Manasseh.

By the time Joshua took the twelve tribes into the Promised Land, all three tribes had an exceedingly large number of cattle. Translated into our language, this means they became wealthy. To become wealthy, we may have to overcome many obstacles in life. People who acquire wealth often work hard and put in long hours. The couch potato lifestyle will not normally produce the full potential of the wealth God has designed for us. Just wishing for great things to happen will not bring anything to pass. God's normal method of bringing wealth into life in biblical language is through seed and harvest. This means God gives us a seed and expects us to plant it, till it, and then harvest the crop planted. In short, He gives us an idea. We then take steps toward bringing that idea to reality. Work is often required and is very closely related to labor and sweat-of-your-brow-type stuff. Wishing should not be considered work, and just wishing brings in very few blessings. If we are searching for a blessing, we should get busy doing something we could be blessed for doing.

Don't get discouraged while working the vision; it may take time. People who are easily discouraged open themselves up to failure. This is a trap designed skillfully and set by the devil to incarcerate those who do not guard their thoughts and speech. We are to control our thoughts and our tongue. To become wealthy, we need a healthy, positive outlook on life.

People with vision talk differently. Years ago I heard a teaching that spoke of three different attitudes or mind sets people have: Closed-minded people usually spend their time talking about other people negatively. Average minded people spend a lot of time talking about things they desire or what others possess. Wealthy minded people usually talk about visions and ideas that help themselves and others. What is the topic of our conversations? It won't take long to figure out which group we are in presently. Fear not; change can happen. It will take discipline, but you can do it. Discipline involves overcoming bad habits with good habits regardless of the circumstances. Remember, it is our circumstances we are trying to change and this change will start with our speech. No shadow of darkness will move until light is placed in its mist. No demon of darkness will move until the power of a positive Holy Spirit-filled word displaces it. In the believer is light; it can only come out of our mouth. "Speak to the mountain, 'Move,' and it will move" (Mark 11:23, KJV). Nothing changes until we say it is going to change. In the last chapter we spoke of speaking toward things. Now we are speaking to ourselves, our flesh, and our character. It is possible to change who we are and how we behave. Start with these words; say them with me: *I feel change coming my way! I'm excited about change! I am ready to embrace change. And I am looking forward to the new friends I'll meet as change comes! I will never go back to the old me! With God I am going to build a new, successful me!*

Without a doubt, we too have accumulated wealth—a wealth of information in our travels in life thus far. We may not feel wealthy by monetary standards, but with God, we are truly wealthy. Wealth is not always about having money. We all learn certain valuable things just from living. It may be time to share with others what we have learned and increase our wealth together.

In our spirit, we may see a work opportunity with another believer. By taking our past experiences and coupling with another individual, both may develop a greater work. This action could prosper both individuals and the Kingdom of God. Great wisdom! The great things from God will always include others. God is really not interested in us becoming a self-serving, self-centered, selfish saint with no interest in the souls or welfare of others. God is in the relationship business. He desires a relationship with us. He teaches unity with others, and His Word speaks of generational investments. That means He is interested in us doing something that will last longer than ourselves. God expects us to be a blessing to the next generation. He also instructs us that we are to be giving. God purposely places people together to accomplish His goal, not necessarily ours. The thought that we get and spend everything on ourselves is not biblical, regardless of the type of wealth we have acquired.

We may need to evaluate the people we are currently involved with. Are they in our best interest? What type of relationship do we have with them? Do these people encourage us in the things of the Lord, or do they pull us down to the methods of poor living? It may be the people we currently hang out with are not as strong as we need in our life right now. By the world's standards, these people may be considered good people, but by the standard God is calling us to, we may have to fellowship with a different circle of people.

If we are bound by any chemical substance or other types of abuse, changing our circle of friends will be absolutely necessary. Our chances of ever being free are closely related to the friends we keep. Who we unite with is very important if we plan to succeed in anything. That principle applies to business and friends. Our walk with the Lord is influenced by the people around us. As we develop our relationship with the Lord, He will encourage us to establish relationships where we are to learn or teach. The position will be revealed as we follow His voice.

It takes vision of better things to come and an overcoming spirit to live toward tomorrow and let go of yesterday. Today we may have been set back by troubles in life, but if we dwell in the down position, we will forfeit our opportunity to any success until we decide to get back up. Keeping our eye on the vision empowers us to treat every setback as a setup opportunity from the Lord. Get over whatever mishap there is in life and use that event as a lesson for the future. We need to get up from whatever has knocked us down and start again. Only God knows where we will end. We must pick and choose our associates carefully. They will influence how our life will end. The choices made yesterday are what we are living today.

The choices today will determine our tomorrows. A better life is all about making the next choice.

It Is Not Always about You

Walking, praying, and listening for God's voice began to calm Rob's spirit. He started thinking, *Maybe this whole marathon run was about something else.* Could the real lesson be hidden in the events that transpired? Maybe it was a test to see if he would give up his own agenda to help a friend. Could it have been his friend needed to see the love of God displayed in some physical way? Rob wondered if the Lord had placed someone along the course that he needed to minister salvation to and, running, he would have missed them. Now Rob was thinking maybe this entire day was designed so that the Lord would receive glory some other way. Rob began to feel a little more encouraged at the prospect of helping someone else. And he was thankful the Lord allowed him to come and see the sights along the way.

He still wanted to finish, but if the Lord had other plans, he would submit to the Lord's leading

Paul said to take every thought captive (2 Corinthians 10:5, KJV). In part, that means we should stop and think before we assume every situation revolves around us. Taking thoughts captive is not just holding them; it should become a short pondering time, a few moments where we weigh the situation against the Word of God. Always remember that He is actively drawing us closer to Him. James 4:7 (KJV) says, "Submit yourselves therefore to God. Resist the devil, and he will flee from you." Much in life can be overcome if we consider the first five words of that verse. Submitting to the Lord in all things takes faith and will always be rewarded. "And the LORD turned the captivity of Job, when he prayed for his friends: also the LORD gave Job twice as much as he had before" (Job 42:10, KJV). In the book of Job, he sits in a pile of ashes for many chapters, mourning the loss of family and possessions. It appears he would have been there for life had he not begun to minister to the friends who first came to minister to him.

Gad's overcoming character may have influenced some members of the other tribes to develop the same trait. Gad was a great fighter with the ability to bounce back. His overcoming spirit and his presence would bring stability to others, especially those living close like the tribe of Rueben and Manasseh.

It's easy to be with people who are gifted to encourage us. Their positive comments make us feel good. There are those in life we receive encouragement from and there are those we are designed to encourage. God often places us in environments where we are able to do both. Since our birth, the Lord has placed us in positions to train us for this moment. The circumstances we are in may not be about us at all. Sometimes we are guilty of only being concerned about ourselves. Someone else may need what God has entrusted to us, but if we are only concerned with ourselves, we may be blind to God's calling at the moment. If we cannot change our circumstances, we might want to look around for others in need. God may be using our circumstances to get us in position to minister to someone else. Like Job, we may find an end to our affliction when we begin to minister to someone else.

It may be a mistake to assume every trial encountered is due to some wrong we have done. A self-condemning attitude can break our joy and cast doubt toward the Lord. Prayer will reveal whether the situation is an attack to fight off or a ministry opportunity to embrace. Having a selfish outlook at life, e.g., thinking everything revolves around us, may be wrong.

Is the issue before us placed in our path by God or the evil one? Adapt a mindset to always minister to someone if the situation permits. If the evil one has attacked, leave no stone unturned in the fight to regain territory, good health, or blessing. If the attack is from Satan, he will leave when he sees us submitting to the Lord's method of living. But be assured, if God has allowed a trial to come, it will not be overcome by shouting at the devil or other people.

Experiencing the freedom of Jesus and seeing others trapped in the same vices we once were in places a burden on our hearts. A word of caution that we must remember: at deliverance, there is no immunity card given that prevents anyone from falling back into old habits. Once delivered from a chemical dependence or other binding lifestyles, we should never go back! Serious prayer time should be spent before attempting to enter into combat with old, familiar spirits. These spirits know very well the weakness of those once trapped. We should minister in this area only if God clearly tells us to. If God does not clearly direct us, don't do it. Never, *never go back!* Never draw near to the old way of life for any reason. God knows what it will take to deliver these people. Our job now is to pray for those who still need deliverance.

We all know of others who are going back and saving souls from the places they were delivered from. We should learn from the mistakes of others. Watch the patterns of those who return. Many good, spirit-filled believers who were once delivered return with the salvation torch to the place they were set free. Sometimes they fall right back into the very thing God delivered them from. God is a big God. He can find those who are not inclined to submit to the vice. There are exceptions. There is always someone to challenge the many who will fail. We must be sure it's God who sends us, not a guilty conscious.

It could be that you are one that was free and now are bound again. In the name of Jesus, get up, run again, and never, ever look back.

FACES LIKE LIONS

*L*ess than five miles to the finish, the Spirit of
God was speaking to Rob.
"Don't give up!"
Rob thought he could walk and still cross the finish
line. Then the Holy Spirit reminded him of the training
he had received months before. Rob looked around to
see if others might be watching. It was almost as if
people near him could hear the Lord's voice as well.
Rob, like most others, was a little self-conscious. He
did not want to be embarrassed. But this adventure
had started with a vision of running this race all the
way through to the finish. He still wanted to finish the
marathon running. So what's a little embarrassment
with so much at stake?

Rob began to throw his arm up and out—first one
hand then the other. He began to punch at the sun
just like he was trained to do. Oh sure, you can believe
he was reluctant. Rob thought he looked like a fool.
He felt like a fool, but down deep, Rob wanted to run

more than he cared about how he looked. He had a goal and wanted to accomplish that goal. Soon he could feel the pull in his legs. He kept punching the sun. Other runners passing by steered far from him. Many veered all the way to the other side of the street. Most likely, they believed he was some kind of crazy man. He kept punching the sun. His mind was fixed toward finishing. What others thought did not matter just now. Rob's vision of finishing the run required him to do what he had never done before. Soon he was running again, not very fast, but he was able to run. His legs were slowly remembering the duty they were trained to do. Sure, he felt a little awkward.

In a few moments, he found another runner to run beside. This runner wore a pace setter. It was a small device worn on his hip. Each time this device clicked, the runners left foot hit the ground. This was a great idea, so Rob decided to keep time for his own step by keeping close to the other runner. Punching the sun worked for Rob. He felt crazy, but the result was fantastic. He was running!

Staying in the race can be easier and more productive when we run with others. Find another believer and help each other maintain pace and direction. Pastors need pastors, women need women, and men need other men who can encourage one another. It is hard when others are against us and harder when we struggle to believe in ourselves, *but* the Word of God will give us faith. Faith will build the vision. With a vision, we now have a goal to run toward. Proverbs 27:17 (KJV) says, "Iron sharpeneth iron; so a man sharpeneth the countenance of his friend." When we partner up with others, we will do better in our Christian walk.

Faith spurs us along to see and do what others may not be able to see or dare to do and vision gives us the courage to continue. By faith we can do anything!

Gadites had faces like lions. Some say they were men who wore full beards. That might be, but it may refer to the character of these men, as well. These men who joined David were men that were fed up with the life they had. They were tired of being broke, bound, and hungry. These men decided one day to take action. Wishful thinking was not accomplishing anything. Waiting on someone else to make a change wasn't happening. Life was not getting any better by complaining. They stood up and decided to fight toward the goal that God had promised them. Years before the men of Gad had crossed into the promised land—a land supposedly filled with milk and honey. These men were not experiencing this promise. For some reason the vision was not coming to pass in their lives. They had to do things differently. They had to take a chance on the young man who was running from King Saul called David. David had a reputation of being a fighter. David had won many battles. So many, in fact, that they sang songs of his exploits. The men of Gad may have heard of his being anointed by the prophet Samuel.. But now this would-be king was on the run. These men of Gad made a life-changing choice. To do nothing was to never have anything better. The situation at present didn't look great, but in their hearts they could see glimpses of possibilities. They went to David and trusted him with their lives and the lives of their children. They would fight the same fights as David with all of their heart. The men of Gad made all of these choices with no guarantees. David proved to be a great leader and King. David watched out for the families of Israel, protecting them and providing for them. These men had faces like lions because their minds were fixed on the vision that God gave them. Their faith was not so much in David as it was in the God David held high before them.

Lion type people have a vision of who they are and what they need. They know that the possibility of being knocked down in life is real. If a blow does knock me down, I am determined to rise again. Just like the men of Gad we are to remain steadfast to the vision and possess an overcoming spirit. The Bible gives us many examples of men and women who were fearless, confident, courageous, and swift. We can have these same qualities when walking with the Lord.

As parents we tell our children, "If you get knocked down, you have to get back up, dust yourself off, and play again. Just because someone bumped into you or you toppled over, it is not the end of life." Get up; there is so much more to do. Using football to illustrate again, when a pro ball carrier is knocked down, two things normally happen. The first is that on the way down, these guys are falling toward the goal line. This makes sense; if they know they're going down, get the ball as close to the goal as possible. Secondly, once they hit the ground, they get up as fast as possible. Never, never, ever rest at the bottom! Well, folks, how about it? It is good advice for children and football players, and it may be good advice to us as well. Get up, dust off, and get back in the race.

There is no race as important as the race of life. To run well, we need to follow a skillful, proven fighter who has a mindset to win. The only one that qualifies is Jesus. It is time to feed on His Word and seek the vision He has for us. It is time for sleeping lions to get up and fight the fight.

The Bible says the least of the captains of Gad were over a hundred soldiers. The greatest was over a thousand (1Chronicles 12:14, KJV). One overcoming Christian with the ability to get back up can lead at least a hundred of those that fall down and stay down. We need to get a hold of this mindset. If we will get up after being knocked down, stay in fellowship with God, stay in church, and continue to live rightly, we may influence hundreds of others to do the same. When we get good at bouncing back after an attack, we may influence thousands. God has great things in store for those who can bounce back. To succeed in anything, it is best to have people that have the ability to get back up. Overcoming all things is possible with Christ Jesus!

Satan and the demons that follow him are our real enemy. They work together to develop a dark cloud of discouragement. The purpose of that dark cloud is to blind us from seeing the true blessing of living with God every day. When the cloud is present, life looks as though we are trapped with no way up or out. That is not true! God always has a way to overcome any circumstance. It's punching the sun! It's punching through the darkness in order to see Jesus and raising our hands, yielding to the only One who can really help us.

We have a King. His name is Jesus. In the eyes of worldly people, many will say they don't see much. Challenge the Scriptures, search the promises, and listen to the testimonies of past victories. Jesus is worthy to be followed. Could you use some of the good things that have heard about? Are you tired of being broke, bound, and discouraged with life? If your answer is yes, then get in the race. Maybe you have been discouraged by the many that have quit. Being around others who lie down and stop running has pulled you down as well. Don't be afraid to change. Wherever you are right now, get your hands up, punch though the darkness toward the Son—*the Son of God*—and begin to run.

To win, to be free, throw your hands up and out! First one hand then the other. Punch through that cloud. Reach for the Son. You will feel the pull and hear His voice, saying, "Come," just like Peter, when we hold on to Jesus. We are sure to walk over what others drown in! He is a proven fighter. He is a winner! With Jesus, you are sure to win!

THE FINISH

Soon Rob could see the finish. Hundreds of supporters were crowded around the finish area watching. The running area up to this point had been both sides of the divided highway. Now it narrowed from four lanes to two. Rob could not see the actual finish line, but by the crowd, he could tell it was near. The road past the crowd appeared to be blocked by the people. Soon he saw United States Marines. They had posted soldiers in two columns, creating a path that narrowed from two lanes even more. Now the way was wide enough for three or maybe four runners to run side by side. Rob felt a rush of excitement as he neared the place that led to the finish line. His body was ready for a rest. It had been a long run. As Rob entered the gauntlet created by the Marines, he did not want to believe what he was seeing. The path lined by the soldiers led *up*—up the hill! The race did not end on the highway. That crowd was not the end. That crowd was the beginning of the end. The place Rob thought was the finish was not the finish at all. Instead it led up a steep hill. As he entered the path, the marines were shouting, "Get the lead out of your shoes! Pick up your feet! Push harder! You can make it! You're almost there! Run, soldier, run! Faster! Faster! Don't quit now!"

At first, Rob thought, *Where have you guys been the past twenty-six miles while we runners were facing the difficulties of the race?* But there was no time for hurling insults back at well-meaning onlookers.

Being at the finish and hearing the people shouting words of encouragement caused Rob's emotions to go crazy. Waves of excitement seemed to race up and down his body each step he took up the hill. At first he wanted to sit down and cry. Next he wanted to jump up and down with laughter. Then he wanted to spin in circles for joy. All these emotions were present at the same time, and he still had yet to cross the finish line, which was only a few yards away. Rob was very surprised at the size of the crowd that had waited to cheer the runners into the finish. At this moment it seemed that everyone in the crowd was cheering just for him. The roar of all the cheering was exhilarating. The first runners had finished long ago, yet these onlookers stayed to encourage others. Rob was excited and thrilled beyond any expectation! Now he could see the real finish line. He could see the gates and the officials that waited by the gates for each runner to finish. Rob was going to finish running twenty-six miles. And he was running! His mind was reeling, and life all around him was a blur. In a few steps, he could say that he had finished!

As Rob entered the gate, he looked up to see the clock indicating the time he crossed the finish line. A camera automatically took his picture and recorded the time. The moment he passed through a gate, a Marine officer placed a marathon finishers' award attached to a ribbon around his neck. Rob came to a stop. He was drinking in the fact that he had finished. He felt so good; it was as if he had received the winner's reward. The officer gently pushed him forward to another officer who wrapped a space blanket around him. This officer pointed Rob toward long tables reserved for those who had overcome the obstacles and finished the race. This area was fenced off so that only the runners were allowed to feast at the tables. In the shade of some large trees were tables mounted up with fresh fruit such as bananas, watermelon, oranges, and melons. Rob headed straight to the melons. As he ate, the glucose in the fruit shot like lightning to the tips of his fingers and toes. His body became electrified, taking in the sugar and carbs it had depleted during the run. The waves of the sweet fruit entering his body made his legs, arms, and hair feel like they were springing straight out. Rob felt like the character you see in the cartoons that has its tail stuck in the electric outlet. Rob could not get enough of the fruit to eat. Rob didn't notice any plates or fancy table settings. Dinnerware could have been present, but Rob didn't notice. What stuck in his mind was that the runners were eating with their hands, pushing the fruit into their bodies and reaching for more as fast as possible. Their bodies were being recharged with each bite. Standing around the tables eating, each runner experienced a comradeship that those who did not run the distance will never know. The words spoken were few, but the message shared was full of emotion. The atmosphere was alive with excitement.

Everyone at the table had finished!

In Luke 15:11-32 (KJV), there is a story about a son who wandered from his home. He lived on his own, did well for a short time, and then life got very difficult. His job didn't pay enough to make ends meet. He hated the food he was able to afford. He knew that the lowest servant in his father's house was living better than he was. He decided to go home and humble himself before his father. His father had been watching the horizon every day, looking for his son. As he was approaching his father's house, to his surprise, his father was running to meet him and rejoiced to have him home again.

Your Father in heaven is watching for you to come back to the Christian walk. He is waiting to run the race of life with you.

My friend, the path to heaven lies before us all. Angels of God line the way on both sides of this narrow path. Oh, how I wish this path were wide and we could run, sit, or live any way we wanted, but it's not wide; it's very narrow, and it is the only path that leads to heaven's table. It is only through Jesus the Christ the Son of the living God and His work on the cross that we will see the Lord's table. He has invited everyone to come and run with Him. He has prepared the celebration table. This table is only for those who run the race and finish with Him. He waits to dine with us. The saints from all time are standing at that table, cheering just for us. Listen, Noah is saying that God will make a way to survive the storm. Abraham is calling to go by faith to where God wants us to be. Joshua is telling of the walls that will fall before us. Peter, Paul, and others are all saying, "Run, run, run! Don't stop! Push harder! You can do it! Get up! Try again! You can make it!"

Life is difficult, but heaven is real and worth the fight. Throw your hands up, punch through to the Son, and His encouraging presence will help you. The Holy Spirit will empower you to run. The vision is before you and is found in your Bible. Your Father that is in heaven stands watching for you daily. He is waiting. The moment He sees you, the command will be shouted. "Quick! Bring out the best robe and put it on my child." The angels of God are waiting to put a robe around you and a crown of life on you for finishing the race , but you must run and not give up. A ring is waiting to be placed on your hand. A celebration meal is being prepared that will be electrifying. We are promised that in heaven there will be a tree with fruits to eat for eternity. I can almost see the saints of all time standing around that tree. They are all eating the sweetest fruit ever grown. They're celebrating that they made it, and all the difficulties in life do not compare to the blessing of being in Jesus's presence. Their immortal bodies are being charged as they take fruit directly off the tree of eternal life. Everyone is praising the One and Only, the true Tree of Life, Jesus the Christ. Whatever you spend running the race toward eternal life will be replenished when you cross over.

My friend, the devil is behind you, scurrying around to take your life. The gates of heaven are open before you. Run! Run to where the God of heaven and all that is good waits for you.

Run! Run! Run! Maintain the vision! You can make it to the finish! You are an overcomer!

The finish was so much more than Rob expected. His vision and dreams were not close to what he experienced. Words are insufficient to express how he felt as he stood before the table eating the fruit. The marathon was one of the hardest things he had ever attempted. Rob would have quit a thousand times had the Lord not been at his side to encourage him. What God has done for Rob, He will do for you!

Run as if your life and the life of others depend on it. It does, and they do!

Keep on running with Jesus!

—Brother Rob

AFTERWORD

"To him that overcometh will I give to eat of the
tree of life, which is in the midst of the paradise
of God. He that overcometh shall not be hurt
of the second death. To him that overcometh
will I give to eat of the hidden manna, and will
give him a white stone, and in the stone a new
name written, which no man knoweth saving
he that receiveth it. And he that overcometh,
and keepeth my works unto the end, to him
will I give power over the nations: And he shall
rule them with a rod of iron; as the vessels of a
potter shall they be broken to shivers: even as
I received of my Father. And I will give him
the morning star. He that overcometh, the same
shall be clothed in white raiment; and I will not
blot out his name out of the book of life, but
I will confess his name before my Father, and
before his angels. Him that overcometh will
I make a pillar in the temple of my God, and
he shall go no more out: and I will write upon

him the name of my God, and the name of the city of my God, which is new Jerusalem, which cometh down out of heaven from my God: and I will write upon him my new name. To him that overcometh will I grant to sit with me in my throne, even as I also overcame, and am set down with my Father in his throne."

Revelation 2:7, 11, 17, 26-28; 3:5, 12, 21

SERVANTS OF THE SAVIOR INT'L MINISTRIES: SOS

*S*ervants of the Savior (SOS) is a ministry of spreading the gospel of Jesus around the world. It was founded by Brother Rob after a trip to Chiapas, Mexico, in 1993. The ministry is comprised of saints that have heard the distress call of those without a Savior. After hearing of others in distress, these saints have determined to respond with the good news of salvation through Jesus. These same saints have caught a vision that they are equipped by God with something that will encourage life in others. Sometimes the good news of hope will include a morsel of food, a warm piece of clothing or something as simple as encouraging words. Each act of kindness builds a bridge for the recipient to see and experience the wonderful love of our Lord Jesus. To give hope to those that have given up hope is the goal and joy of these great men and women of God.

I want to encourage you to do something for someone else that will brighten their day. As soon as you begin putting others first, you will find a deep sense of warmth that will bless you. Brother Rob and Sister Ellie have devoted their lives to helping others. We would love to have you as one of our partners in prayer, work, and support of SOS ministries. SOS distress signals are being broadcasted all around you. You can be a responder to the souls in distress.

You may find us on the web at www.servantsofthesavior.net. There you will find information on where they have been and what they are doing. You are welcome and encouraged to get involved.